VANISHING LIGHTS

VANISHING LIGHTS

CHRIS MILLS

On the frontispiece:
2nd order double flashing light,
Gannet Rock, 1905.
National Archives. Neg. # C139288

ISBN 0-88999-487-0
Published 1992
Second printing December 1992

LANCELOT PRESS LIMITED, Hantsport, Nova Scotia
Office and production facilities situated on Highway No. 1,
1/2 mile east of Hantsport.

Mailing address:
P.O. Box 425, Hantsport, Nova Scotia B0P 1P0

ACKNOWLEDGEMENT
This book has been published with the
assistance of The Canada Council.

CONTENTS

Acknowledgements 7

1. **A Guiding Light** 11

2. **A Maritime Tradition** 21

3. **Cross Island:** 42
   First Light

4. **Seal Island:** 66
   Seals, Shipwrecks & Sheep

5. **Machias Seal Island:** 98
   Christmas and Controversy

6. **Gannet Rock:** 122
   The Rock

Epilogue 155

Notes 159

Source Material 165

ACKNOWLEDGEMENTS

To Robert (Bob) Boudreau of the Canadian Coast Guard Base Saint John for his unfailing willingness to locate documents and photographs, Ann Romeril and Alison Hale of the National Archives of Canada, Wilfred Tucker, Dave Smith of the Canadian Coast Guard Base Dartmouth, Nova Scotia, Coast Guard Pilot Jack Jardine for the transportation to and from the lights and for the aerial photo opportunities, Wendy Dathan of the Grand Manan Museum, Roger Nickerson of the Barrington Historical Society.

To the lightkeepers — James R. Smith for his invaluable research assistance, Walter and Louise Goodwin, Brian and Sherrill Stoddard, George and Ethel Locke, Doug and Deborah Daggett, James and Mary Nickerson, D. Wickerson Lent, Peter Coletti, Don Denton.

To Ernest H. (Rip) Irwin for his interest in lighthouses and his support and friendship over the past six years, Anne, Eric and Karen Mills for editorial and creative input, Chris Bennett for generous assistance with computer hardware and software, the staff of Black's, Bayer's Road, Halifax, Margaret Messenger, Elaine Maker, Barna B. Norton, Ronald Spinney, Carman MacArthur, Phyllis Wilcox, Doug and William Pope for their interest in my project from the beginning.

NEW BRUNSWICK

P.E.I.

MAINE

Saint John

Île Haute

Minas Basin

NOVA SCOTIA

Deer Island

The Wolves
Campobello Island

BAY OF FUNDY

Halifax

Grand
Manan
Island

Sambro Island 175

Machias Seal
Island

Gannet
Rock

Lunenburg

East Ironbound

Cross Island

Brier
Island

ATLANTIC OCEAN

Yarmouth

Cape Forchu

Argyle

McNutt Island
Cape Roseway 1788

Seal Island

oSt. Paul's Island
Light closed 1991

Sydney ◁ Scatarie
Island
Louisburg
First light in
Canada 1733

°Country Island

DEDICATION

This book is dedicated to the good friends I have made on the lights — lightkeepers, fishermen and coastal dwellers, and to the memory of Ethel Marie Locke 1944-1990.

Early lighthouse oil lamp.
E.H. Irwin photo.

Second order lens used at Seal Island: b/w 1902-1978. Now a part of the Seal Island Light Museum in Barrington, N.S. *Chris Mills photo.*

ONE

A Guiding Light

LIGHTHOUSES HAVE been a part of my life for as long as I can remember. It is hard to say how or when my interest in these beacons began — perhaps in May 1965, when I was five months old, as my mother carried me up the spiral stairs of the great lighthouse at Cape Hatteras, North Carolina. As a child I was fearfully fascinated by the bellow of the foghorn at the lightstation on Brier Island's western shore and dizzied by the seemingly endless flights of iron ladders to the top of the lighthouse.

Each trip to the lighthouse was an adventure and, even at the age of six, I appreciated the tall red and white banded tower and its surrounding white buildings, sheds and walkways set against the backdrop of sea and rock. There was something compelling in the sight of a cluster of red and white buildings overlooking the sea and the slow turn of the light in the lantern as darkness fell.

On foggy days the clockwork grunts of the foghorn passed the minutes and hours. The white bungalows and one-and-a-half-storey frame houses were the same on most stations, with sleepy blinds, like eyelids, pulled halfway down sash windows.

The sheds and boathouses sometimes displayed giant maple leaves on the doors, evidence of Canadian keepers' pride. Wooden walkways with red and white railings connected station buildings over uneven ground, and a tall white flagpole flew another maple leaf, snapping in the breeze. This was the Canadian lightstation, and although on the east coast it lives mainly in memory, the sight will always be in my mind.

And the smell! There is a smell that is peculiar to all lighthouses: a combination of diesel oil, paint, newly mown grass and the ever present odour of the sea. Even today when I notice it, I'm taken back twenty years to those first lighthouse visits. Lightkeeping has changed greatly in the last two decades: most lighthouses are now automated and stand alone on the shorelines and islands, with keepers gone and houses and sheds razed. But the smell remains. It lingers amongst the empty, rusting fuel tanks by the shore, in the dusty basements of remaining abandoned dwellings and in the entryways of old light towers.

My attachment to lighthouses has been enhanced by living and travelling around Atlantic Canada for twenty-five years. I have lived on St. Margaret's Bay in Nova Scotia for much of that time and have spent summers motorboating, sailing and fishing. As I grew up, my parents' interest in birdwatching and hiking enabled me to spend time in coastal Nova Scotia and to become familiar with the shorelines and islands that once supported families and small communities. I was always intrigued by the contrasts I saw between the isolation of remote areas and the civilization of settlements.

I spent summers on the basalt island at the end of Digby Neck and came to love the shores that bore the brunt of winter gales and summer fog. It was there on Brier Island that I built my first lighthouse at the age of six. I build the two-foot structure with pieces of driftwood and lobster trap slats and topped it with a red trouble light. I insisted that it be kept by the cottage facing south and that it be turned on each night so the boats in St. Mary's Bay could navigate safely. That little tower survives to this day.

Looking back, it is amazing to me that I am now a keeper myself, on Gannet Rock, twenty-five nautical miles northwest of Brier island. In retrospect it would seem natural that my long-time interest should lead to my employment as a keeper, but even now as the foghorn blasts above my head I find it hard to believe that I am here. I wrote this sitting in the kitchen of a dwelling attached to a lighthouse on a minute lump of conglomerate at the northern entrance to the Bay of Fundy. Over the muted roar of the kemac cookstove, the lighthouse generators rumbled, and overhead the beam of the main light swung in never ending circles. Its single flash every six seconds tells ships and fishing vessels to stay clear — the waters around the Murr Ledges are dangerous at the best of times.

From Grand Manan, the jumble of volcanic rock and light tower provide the only break in an otherwise featureless seascape. On the station, the ordered routine of lightkeeping sets the pace for the month, while outside the environment constantly changes. The lighthouse weathers massive seas, fog and wind. But in the dwelling everything is normal, like any house on the mainland.

Through the double-sash window in the living room is the ocean, sparkling brilliant in the sun, or flat and grey in the fog, sometimes rolling in huge swells, lashing spray on the glass. You almost take the sea for granted, except when fierce winds and spring tides whip up dwelling-sized waves and send spray slashing across the windows. After a good blow, everything is covered by a crystalline layer of salt. Sometimes the wind comes up out of nowhere and you rush outside to secure flying buckets, brooms, mops and ladders.

As lightkeepers we are surrounded by the sea, but unlike fishermen and other mariners we live and work on an immobile chunk of land. Though subject to the vagaries of weather, we are affected by it in different ways. On islands, mowing and painting days are carefully selected, as even a few moments of rain or a sudden squall can create interruption. On Gannet, shutters are closed when the wind is forecast at forty knots or more, to protect windows from the incredible force of air and water. But regardless of the weather, the keepers go about their routine, contained by wooden and concrete walls on a speck of land in the midst of fog, storm and tide.

This is my second shift on the rock and probably one of the last for all time. Gannet is due to be destaffed in the not too distant future, and with the departure of the last keeper more than 160 years of human habitation on the rock will end. It is ironic that my opportunity to experience this unique lifestyle has come at this time of lighthouse automation. With most full-time keepers retired or redeployed, it has been difficult to find people to fill in on the remaining staffed stations with no promise of continued employment or long-term benefits. I remember going to the Canada Employment Centre in Halifax

The author with his first lighthouse and fog alarm, Brier Island, 1971. *Anne Mills photo.*

at the age of sixteen to enquire about lightkeeping positions and being told that no one was hired anymore and, anyway, weren't all the lights automated now? Eight years later, two months after my twenty-fourth birthday, I got my first posting as a relief assistant lightkeeper.

In the intervening three years, I have worked on lighthouses that had for years provided invaluable service to steamers, schooners and fishing vessels. Although I am unhappy to see the final results of a program of automation begun some twenty-five years ago by the Canadian Coast Guard, I feel extremely lucky to have had the chance to work on the lights and experience for myself this solitary but fulfilling way of life.

Though it's true I have never "lit up" the main light at sundown or started the compressors when the fog crept in, I have shared in the experiences common to all lightkeepers: the routine, weather reports and radio schedules, the chores — painting, pumping oil and water, cleaning lantern windows — and the loneliness.

Not that it's always lonely on the lights; feelings of isolation are not so much a result of being physically separate from society, but of one's state of mind. It takes a certain kind of person, or perhaps a certain mind set, to spend weeks or months in isolation with limited contact with "civilization." Time can pass slowly, especially during the winter months, and it becomes necessary to pace activities so that nothing is done too fast or all at once. I found the change in tempo difficult to deal with at first, being accustomed to the relative bustle of mainland life, but after a time I found that it was possible to slow down and at the same time remain productive.

This book is a record of my experiences as a lightkeeper on four islands in Nova Scotia and New Brunswick in a period that could be called the "fading gleam" of lightkeeping in Canada. Though thirty-odd stations in British Columbia and thirty in Newfoundland continue to be staffed, it is unlikely that they will remain so for many more years. Lighthouses, like glass milk bottles and corner drugstores, have fallen victim to progress in the push-button age of fax machines, loran and satellites. Nonetheless, lights and their keepers still have a venerable place in Maritime history, having formed a network of coastal observation and marine rescue for more than two centuries.

Despite similar routines and standardized equipment, each lightstation has its own character, and every island has a singular atmosphere and sense of identity. On Cross Island, sitting at Lunenburg Harbour's broad mouth, I met Smiths and Levys and DeMones. The island had once been home to fishermen and their families, and I was able to learn of the early settlement of the place through my lightkeeping partners, George and Ethel Locke. They also told me of strange presences and unexplained sightings, stirring in my mind images of ghosts that would linger as I watched the last helicopter evacuation of what would soon be a deserted island.

On Seal Island, eighteen miles west of the southwest tip of Nova Scotia, I had the opportunity to explore and reacquaint myself with a place that I had been visiting since childhood. I came to appreciate the light's role on the history of the area and the feelings of local people toward the island and its place in their lives. On Seal it was possible to spend time with visitors — fishermen, birdwatchers and tourists — and to stretch one's legs and get away from the station to walk the woods and shorelines. The wooded shores, grassy dunes and quiet clearings offered an infinite number of activities away from the lightstation and I never felt physically isolated there.

On Machias Seal Island, the "seabird republic," I learned of the island's importance to both the United States and Canada, and of the controversy that will undoubtedly allow it to remain the last staffed island lighthouse in the Maritimes. Machias Seal also introduced me to the constraints of living and working in a limited physical space. The island's fifteen-acre area and distance from the mainland made it seem so much more remote than the larger islands.

The engine room at Seal Island, circa.1920. *Courtesy Mary Nickerson.*

But Machias was just a stepping stone for me to the black and white pillar on Gannet Rock. Gannet has no trees, no grass and very little space. A combination of physical and social isolation make the rock perhaps the most interesting station on which to work. Less than one-half an acre provides room enough for a tower, dwelling, fuel bunker and helicopter pad, but no more. A twenty-two-lap run around the concrete deck surrounding the tower and house equals one mile and is at best a tedious way to remain fit. Living in close quarters with another keeper also presents unique difficulties — after a while you run out of things to say, and if you don't get along, well, it is no place to be. Nevertheless, we are in constant contact with local fisherman on the VHF radio and I have gotten to know many of the scallop, lobster and herring fishermen who have for many years depended on the services of Gannet's keepers for on-the-spot weather reports.

I am proud to have worked in a profession that was for so many years crucial to the safety of seafarers, but much of my interest in lighthouses and lightkeeping has been, in a sense, less practical. If I had been a lightkeeper fifty or even twenty-five years ago, much of my time would have been taken up with the involved maintenance of station equipment and the vigilance that was essential to the efficient operation of a lighthouse before automation. Today I have more time to contemplate lighthouse life. Late twentieth-century technology has not only made manually operated equipment obsolete, it has lessened the need for the flashing beacons themselves. Given this overall reduction in responsibility for both the light and its attendants, I have had time to reflect on my attachment to lighthouses and to live a way of life that has appealed to me for so long.

Much of the material for this book is drawn from my lighthouse journals, in which I have detailed my day-to-day existence as a lightkeeper and my feelings toward the lighthouse "way of life." There was much to record: the physical aspects of the islands and lightstations, history, the people with whom I worked and whom I met, and the sunsets, sunrises, smells, storms, arguments, stories, ghosts, wildlife and regimen of chores. Although much of what I have written deals with the routine that formed such a large part of each day, the dominant theme in my journals is my profound interest in the whole idea of the lighthouse. The concept of a light on a small island or a craggy rock appeals to me. Every aspect of the structure of the lightstation and the life within draws me to it.

Many of the observations from my journals are vignettes of experiences that struck me as significant at the time. Indeed, most are as fresh in my mind now as they were when they occurred. I noticed the way the last rays of sunlight gave the scraggly trees on Seal Island a beautiful golden glow just before dusk, and I listened to the stovepipe-rattling buzz of the foghorn on Gannet Rock. The comfortable feeling of talking to a friend on Grand Manan on the VHF radio while the seas threw spray on the windowpanes has stayed with me, and so has the excitement of the first flash of a lighthouse from a descending helicopter. All of these simple incidents, and hundreds of others, have formed a great and important part of my lighthouse experience. To have the opportunity to work as a lightkeeper and have the time to savour every aspect of the job was my dream, and I feel privileged to have spent at least a few years of my life as an island keeper.

Louisbourg lighthouse, 1987. *Chris Mills photo*.

TWO

A Maritime Tradition

MARITIME LIGHTHOUSES were the first built in Canada. The French and British initially established lights to guide their ships into port and to benefit trade with the American colonies and West Indies. In 1731 the French began construction of a lighthouse at the eastern side of Louisbourg harbour and on April 1, 1734, its light shone for the first time.

North America's oldest existing lighthouse continues to send out its rays from Sambro Island, although its keepers are now gone. Financed by a lottery and a tax on spirits, it was constructed of stone and completed in 1760. Funds for maintenance of the light and its keeper were raised by a tax levied on ships entering Halifax Harbour. When the sloop *Granby* and all hands were lost on the Sambro ledges not long after the light was established, the Royal Navy's commander-in-chief in Halifax stated that the wreck had been caused by the poor light kept at Sambro, and that ships "are frequently, nay, almost constantly obliged to fire at the lighthouse to make them show a light." By the next year a better ventilation system had much improved the quality of light shown from the lighthouse, ending the need to attract the lightkeeper's attention with heavy artillery!

A signal station was established on Sambro in the late eighteenth century, and in 1808 the commander-in-chief at Halifax issued these instructions to naval ships entering the harbour so they might ascertain the conditions of visibility around the island:

> Question: Is it clear within the lighthouse — One Gun and 3 Minutes after 2 Guns quick.
>
> Answer: Yes — One Gun and 3 Minutes after 2 Guns quick.
> No — One Gun Only.
>
> There being only one gun at the Lighthouse 2 Guns will not be so quick as those from the Ships.[1]

By 1833 a detachment of artillerymen was stationed on the island, along with two twenty-four-pounders to be used as signal and fog guns. Later, another gun was placed on the island, and in the late 1980s there were still two cannon and part of the third near the base of the lighthouse.

In 1988 I visited Sambro Island with my friend and lighthouse research colleague, Ernest "Rip" Irwin. I was nearing the end of my fourth year at King's College in Halifax and I was coming uncomfortably close to the submission deadline for my honours dissertation. I really didn't have two days to spare, but the chance to stay two nights on Sambro Island, one week before the station would be destaffed, was too appealing to pass up. We travelled to the island on the Sambro Village-based Coast Guard lifeboat and ended up staying not two but three days, delayed by high winds and rough seas. We spent our time interviewing the keepers, making sketches and taking notes and photographs. In the evenings we all sat in the crowded Fairservice living room, surrounded by packing boxes and crates, talking about the family's experiences on the island and their plans upon leaving the place that had been their home for more than two decades.

During our second evening on the island, the Fairservices

Two of the fog cannon remaining on Sambro Island. *Chris Mills photo.*

Left: Acetylene fog gun house, Green Island, 1940. *Canadian Coast Guard, St. John, N.B.* Right: Sambro Island lighthouse, c. 1900. *Public Archives of N.S.*

Old warehouse and lighthouse, Sambro Island, 1988. Interior was remodelled in 1987 for a Highliner Fish TV commercial. *Chris Mills photo.*

told us of Sambro's resident ghost, Alex Alexander. Over the years several strange incidents involving Alex had occurred on the island and, as Rip and I listened to John and Marjorie's tales, we both wondered if we might be lucky enough to catch a glimpse of the infamous spirit. Later that night, after we had all turned in, I heard a noise in the living room downstairs. There were three of us in the assistant keeper's house, each in our respective rooms, lights out. Earlier in the day we had looked over some nautical charts, spread over the living room floor. As I lay in my sleeping bag I heard someone rustling through the charts, as though they were searching for one in particular. After a few minutes the noise stopped and all was quiet — no footsteps, no breathing. I lay quietly for a while, listening to the wind outside and then got up and walked to the head of the stairs. The lights were on below, but nothing stirred. I returned to bed and lay awake for an hour or so, listening for more activity downstairs, but I heard nothing for the rest of the night.

The next day I asked Rip and the lightkeeper if they had been up during the night at all, looking at the charts. No, they said, they had been asleep with their doors closed. Perhaps I should have gone downstairs that night. I might have had the last glimpse ever of Double Alex. A week later, John, Marjorie and Kelly Fairservice left the island for good, taking with them remembrances of twenty-four years of good and bad times, and memories of Alex Alexander's presence.

The third light to be built in Nova Scotia (and Canada) was established at Cape Roseway on McNutt's Island at the entrance to Shelburne Harbour in 1788 and lighted in September 1792. Alexander Cocken, the keeper, ran a school of marine navigation for young men at the lighthouse for a quarter of a century to supplement his small salary. In thick weather, as was done on Sambro, he fired a twenty-four-pounder at regular intervals to guide vessels into port.

Cannons were used to warn vessels of islands and rocks in some locations even before lighthouses were established. On

Green Island, near Yarmouth, a caretaker fired a cannon every 15 minutes in thick weather; not until 1964 was a combination lighthouse and fog alarm built. On Cross Island, a signal cannon was rescued by the keepers in the 1960s after it had been thrown over a cliff below the station. It remained at the lighthouse until removed from the island shortly after by the Coast Guard. On McNutt's Island, a cannon used in the early nineteenth century as a fog signal was unearthed by provincial highway workmen who were building a road on the island. According to Otis Orchard, who kept the Cape Roseway light from 1920 to 1956, this cannon had been placed on the island many years before the light was established; it had been primed with one pound of gunpowder and fired every half hour to assist vessels in making Shelburne Harbour in foggy weather. In 1966 Harry VanBuskirk and his two assistants brought the cannon on its teak carriage to the station and placed it near the lighthouse and adjacent to its modern-day counterpart, the diaphone.

Although steam whistles and trumpets[2] had replaced fog cannons by the late nineteenth century, explosive fog signals continued in use until the 1960s. Just before the turn of the century a bomb rocket was installed on Sambro Island that was fired every twenty minutes in thick weather. Later, an acetylene gun was introduced that sounded once every minute, and this was used until replaced by a diaphone in 1963.

In the late 1950s the Cape Roseway lighthouse burned after being hit by lightning and was replaced by a concrete tower. Beginning with the country's first beacon at Louisbourg, which was gutted in 1736, countless lighthouses have been levelled by fire. Excepting the stone towers at Louisbourg, Sambro and Cape Roseway (and even two of these fell prey to the ravages of fire), most nineteenth-century Canadian lighthouses were constructed of wood. The same material that was plentiful and cheap to use was also easily caught alight. Without access to proper firefighting equipment, many lighthouses burned to the ground while keepers and their families watched helplessly.

Fire was a constant risk in the days of open-flame lights, whether they burned seal oil or vapourized kerosene. According to Edward F. Bush in *The Canadian Lighthouse*, the first lighthouse at Louisbourg burned as a result of a faulty lantern design which allowed combustible elements to be ignited by the sperm oil-fed wicks. The second lighthouse, designed to be fireproof, was not proof against the cannon fire that damaged it severely during the second British seige in 1758. The structure was not replaced until 1842, and some eighty years later, this third lighthouse, made of wood, succumbed to the fate of the first.

Later lighthouses burned when kerosene apparatuses caught fire. More than two centuries after the first Louisbourg tower was gutted, a new concrete tower was completed on Brier Island's western shore, replacing an original tower. During the winter of 1944 a fire that began when a can of oil was spilled in the lantern engulfed the wooden structure within minutes. The keeper only just escaped with his life, to watch the tower burn to the ground.

Other lights were struck by lightning. Machias Seal Island keeper Reg Smith noted that over the years he had seen much electrical activity around the towers at Cape Sable, Green Island and Machias — blueish streaks dancing around the lanterns. In January 1870 the East Ironbound light was struck, and within hours the structure had been levelled. The same fate befell the light on Whitehead Island near Argyle, Yarmouth County, in 1951. Fourteen-year-old Ronald Spinney, the son of the lightkeeper, was alone on the island one evening in October when a thunder squall struck. It was dusk and he was washing dishes in the kitchen of the combination lighthouse-dwelling, having finished lighting the main lamp for the evening. As he stood near the sink, a bolt of lightning struck the ground near the lighthouse. Ron remembers thinking "I hope the light doesn't get hit!" just before the second bolt hit the structure. He couldn't be sure if the lightning had struck the bottom or the top of the tower, but near a basement window was a hole in the ground where the bolt had either entered or exited the building. Ron rushed up the tower to check the light, and although some plaster had been blown off the walls, he could detect no sign of fire.

Returning to the kitchen, he finished his dishes and then once again climbed the tower to assess the damage. By this time he could hear the flames inside the walls of the structure. Without any firefighting equipment on hand, he had no hope of extinguishing the blaze, so he set about removing his family's possessions from the burning building and then went outside "and watched 'er burn." Some three hours later he was picked up by a fishing boat from Abbot's Harbour and taken ashore. The lighthouse, the Spinney's home, burned to the ground.

Despite Imperial concern with shipping and navigation in the British North American colonies, it was not until the mid-nineteenth century that lighthouse construction really took off on the east coast of Canada. The lights which had originally been built for colonial shipping now began to serve the needs of local traders and fishermen. Through petitions, local residents and shipping interests urged government to establish lights, which would be of "great advantage to the persons engaged in the coasting trade" and provide safe guidance for "vessels seeking a harbour during the stormy seasons of the year."

One of the first lights on the southwest coast of Nova Scotia was established in 1840 at Cape Forchu. Today a modern concrete tower guides ferry and fishing boat traffic into this port, which was once one of the busiest in the Atlantic region. Unlike most lighthouses in the Maritimes, Yarmouth's beacon was evolved to keep pace with the same technological advances that have removed the keepers from most of its brother and sister stations. It is a central monitoring facility, where the vital components — main lights, fog detectors, fog horns, emergency generators, emergency lights and fuel supply

Cape Forchu. "Applecore" design, replacing the original wooden octagonal tower in 1962. *Chris Mills photo.*

levels — of twenty-two automated lightstations are monitored and controlled by a team of four lightkeepers, twenty-four hours a day, seven days a week. These modern-day lighthouse attendants stand nine- and fifteen-hour watches in front of a flickering video terminal, monitoring changes of state in the operation of lighthouse equipment and maintaining radio communications with Coast Guard helicopters and service crews.

The overnight watch, from five in the evening to eight the next morning can be a long one, especially when the weather is changeable. As the fog moves in and out, twenty foghorns (two of the stations have no fog signals) turn on and off, sending airborne impulses to the computer in the watch room where a warbling electronic alarm demands the acknowledgement of the keeper on duty. Thunderstorms and power failures play havoc with the system, causing a stream of faults, interrogations and acknowledgements to be recorded on the computer printout.

On several occasions I spent time with the keepers at Cape Forchu while I waited for the weather to clear so a helicopter could get across the bay to take me to Gannet Rock. Acting Principal Keeper Walter Goodwin and his wife Louise introduced me to the monitoring system, and to the warmth of lighthouse life. Prior to their posting at Cape Forchu, they had lived for eleven years on Whitehead Island, near Argyle. It was a change to come ashore to the nine to five schedule of the Cape, but they were able to live at the lighthouse while spending off-duty time at their home in Argyle Sound. Walter retired early in 1992 and, although Louise continues to work as a keeper at Cape Forchu, it is uncertain how much longer she and the other keepers will be required. Technology may soon catch up with these attendants, as plans are in hand to move the monitoring station to another Coast Guard facility. And so the care of lighthouses will pass out of the hands of lightkeepers entirely.

Some twenty years after the light at Cape Forchu was lit,

lighthouses at Boar's Head, Cape St. Mary's, and Bunker, Pease's, Candlebox and Whitehead islands were established and all of these lights remain in service today. By the early twentieth century the east coast of Canada had a comprehensive network of visual and audio aids to navigation, including lights, horns, whistles, buoys and daymarks. Almost all of these beacons and sound signals required constant human supervision and hence was born the need for lightkeepers. Except in the cases of some small harbour lights, most lighthouses had attendants who lived on site, often with their families.

Remote islands and headlands became enclaves of civilization. Most lighthouse families, out of necessity, raised crops and livestock on the barren land in order to survive. Often soil was brought to rockbound sites for the purpose of growing vegetables and flowers. On already populated islands, lightstations became social and communications centres. Keepers patrolled beaches and kept an eye peeled for trouble in the surrounding waters. Although only a handful of lightstations were officially designated as lifesaving stations, all lightkeepers were lifesavers on those occasions of dire necessity when vessels went down in nearby waters.

A large community of fishermen and mariners depended on keepers for light, horn and assistance in distress. As late as 1990 the lightkeepers on Seal Island, Nova Scotia, were the unofficial watchmen of the island. They kept an eye on fishermen's shacks, charged batteries, patched punctured tires, kept food frozen for fishermen and visitors, supplied the odd replacement part or piece of equipment, relayed local weather conditions on the VHF and in general provided whatever service they could to people on and around the island. This was also the case at countless other islands.[3]

When lighthouses became automated, the keepers were often the final residents of islands like Scatarie, Seal, MacNutt's and Cross that had lost all or most of their year-round residents. In some instances, keepers left before residents. On one island in New Brunswick, "the lighthouse, seemingly a fixture on the island, was shut down and burned — and with the demise of the lighthouse, that sustaining beacon of island life, the last islanders ... packed their belongings ... and struggled to put down new roots" on the mainland. Nevertheless, lighthouses remain on many islands that have been long abandoned, as a reminder of the keepers, fishermen and farmers who settled, lived and finally left.

Islands foster a different type of life than on the mainland for the people who inhabit them. Physical isolation has necessitated close ties amongst island dwellers, and in some respects present-day communities are like extended families where everyone helps one another out. With increasing urbanization in the twentieth century, the character of islands has changed as populations have decreased or people have left completely to find work and settle on the mainland. Nevertheless, some of the larger outposts continue to thrive and prosper as their people adapt to changing times. Islands such as Brier, Grand Manan and Big Tancook are a testament to this. Smaller islands like Pictou and East Ironbound continue to hold populations of a few families.

In my experience, I have found islanders and inhabitants of remote mainland communities to be friendly, welcoming and hospitable people who are resourceful by necessity. In essence, islands are mini-environments where the constraints of space and accessibility combine to produce a way of life both caring and close, dramatic and hostile. This observation applies to lightstation life as well. The keepers who lived and worked in these remote areas were close both physically and emotionally. As well as sharing good times and helping one another, they weathered gales and social conflicts. "Life ... is strictly governed by storms and tides as well as by the unavoidable interaction of humans confined to a limited space."

Undoubtedly this last point is one of the most important

for the people who have lived and worked on the lights. Keepers who did not get along had their problems — some came close to killing one another and others engaged in only the most necessary interactions for the running of the station while living next to each other on tiny islands. When you see the same person for weeks or months on end, the old saying that "familiarity breeds contempt" can become a dangerous reality. Petty arguments, individual habits and cabin fever can combine to produce explosive situations which are often difficult to walk away from, especially on an isolated rock in the middle of a howling easterly gale!

Nevertheless, most keepers get along well enough to avoid lasting enmities. Significantly, the work performed by modern keepers is fairly equal, with the distinction between principal keepers and assistants being more a formality than a necessity. In the past, assistants were hired by the main lightkeeper and paid by him, while he took complete responsibility for the running of the station. Since 1959, junior keepers have been hired as civil servants as well and thus have achieved a more equal footing with principal keepers. A good friend to whom I was assistant for almost a year said, "I won't ask you to do anything on the station that I wouldn't do myself. As far as I am concerned we share the work equally. But remember, after me you come first!"

Perhaps in some ways lightkeepers of the past were less isolated than now, as they did not live in a time when urban amenities were considered the norm and, indeed, expected. Today it is hard to believe that families grew and prospered on tiny islands and headlands and could survive without the benefit of churches, schools and hospitals. Lightkeeping was a complete way of life for keepers and their families, and they accepted the drawbacks of island living as part of the experience. Today VHF telephones, satellite dishes, TVs and VCRs bring the outside world to lightstations, while submarine cables and thundering diesel generators provide power for these as well as other amenities — stoves, refrigerators and deep freezers. Relief and supply visits by helicopters have reduced isolation at stations and have greatly decreased the uncertainty of travel to and from lightstations. Nevertheless, most choppers cannot fly in high wind and conditions of reduced visibility, and even today stations can be cut off from the outside world for weeks when bad weather sets in.

Lighthouses hold a fascination for many people. A slender white tower rising from the craggy rocks of a headland is a romantic image, symbolizing safety and security for those at sea. For years tourists have delighted in climbing tower stairs to the magnificent view from the lantern and balcony.

Looking north from the tower on Machias Seal Island. *Chris Mills photo.*

Most keepers have been forthcoming with tales of storms and rescues, and both tourists and seafarers have come to identify lightkeepers as part of maritime tradition. Keepers and their families were the warmth behind the lights, and mariners sensed this as they headed out to sea or approached safe harbour. But despite the importance of a human presence at the lighthouses, the increasing use of communications and navigation technology decreased mariners' reliance on beacons and foghorns. By the late 1960s the Department of Transport began a program of semi-automation which was to reduce staff requirements on lightstations and ultimately remove all keepers. This program was envisaged to be completed in the mid-1970s, but it was not until ten years later that the greatest reductions in keepers were made on the east coast of Canada.

Between 1980 and 1991, more than seventy lightstations in the Maritime Provinces were destaffed, including forty-eight in the period from January 1986 to December 1988 alone. This was the largest cut ever, and most of the remaining staffed stations were to be closed by 1991. In most cases, meetings were held prior to automation of lights by the Coast Guard to discuss plans with marine interests. But many meetings were poorly attended and consequently the lights were destaffed without delay. Although mariners, especially fishermen, complained amongst themselves, no concerted effort was made to slow the automation process. In British Columbia, where the volume of coastal commercial and pleasure boat traffic is greater than on the east coast, political pressure and complaints from users of aids to navigation has resulted in a temporary halt to the automation program.

In Nova Scotia and New Brunswick, four lightstations remain staffed, two of these being central stations that remotely monitor and control the automated lights, and the remaining stations have resident attendants. The lightkeepers' work has been pared down to general maintenance; they are now essentially groundskeepers.

A look through the phone listings for Grand Manan reveals scores of names associated with lighthouses in the area. Fleets, Greens, Guptills, Ingalls, Ingersolls, Tates, Wilcoxes and Wilsons have given years of service on Gannet Rock, Machias Seal Island, Southwest Head, Long Point, Swallowtail, Big Duck and Long Eddy. In 1992, Grand Mananers continued to work on the two remaining staffed lighthouses in the Fundy region.

Fathers, mothers, sons, daughters, uncles, aunts and friends have shared lightkeeping responsibilities from generation to generation. In most coastal communities around the Maritimes, people know or knew someone who was a lightkeeper. On the west point of Scatarie Island, near Main-a-Dieu, Eliza Campbell kept the light for twenty-one years and raised a family after her husband died; her son Tommy worked for a time as keeper at the east light. Mary and Jim Nickerson were keepers on Seal Island where Mary's forebears had kept the light since 1831. In 1990 Jim was one of the last lightkeepers on the island. On East Ironbound Island, Paul Finck was the last lightkeeper in 1990, ending the family tradition of lightkeeping on the island begun by his grandfather in 1930.

Kelly Fairservice Brown grew up on Sambro Island at the entrance to Halifax Harbour. In 1988 she was the last keeper on the station where her family had lived and worked for twenty-four years. Kelly told me that life on Sambro had been special, and although she missed friends and social activities ashore, the island had enabled her to become independent and confident. "How many kids can drive a tractor, chart a course and dock a boat without doing too much damage, at age twelve?" she asked me.

The teenage years had been difficult, she remembers, especially when friends were socializing and partying on the weekends. On a number of occasions she had watched from the isolation of the island her friends' bonfires on Crystal Crescent Beach and questioned the profession that had taken her family from everyday life ashore to a barren granite island. Whenever

Lighthouse children on Seal Island. *Both photos courtesy Mary Nickerson.*

Kelly spent any amount of time ashore though, she grew homesick for Sambro Island. A year after leaving the lightstation, she told me that family bonds had been tight, and that living so close to the sea and nature had given her a special appreciation for a way of life that was both unforgiving and rewarding.

For many like Kelly, the station was not only a place to work, it was also a home. Traditionally, lighthouse families shared in all of the chores necessary for the operation of the station. Horses, cattle, sheep, chickens, grains and vegetables were raised for food. To read Evelyn Richardson's *We Keep A Light*, one would think that the Richardsons did indeed live on a farm and not on a island lightstation. Nevertheless, the important task of maintaining the light and associated buildings took precedence. The light was lit at sunset and extingished at sunrise. At most lightstations in the nineteenth and early twentieth centuries, light was provided by oil-burning lamps.

In the early nineteenth century, whale and seal oils were burned, often giving a smoky light of low intensity. In 1846, Abraham Gesner, a physician from Cornwallis, Nova Scotia, devised a method of distilling "coal oil," or kerosene, from solid hydrocarbons. Gesner's invention had a profound impact on lighthouse lighting systems worldwide, to say nothing of the petroleum industry in general. Kerosene produced a much higher intensity light than whale or seal oils and burned more efficiently, resulting in a reduced consumption of fuel. In many lighthouses, a lamp (or lamps) similar to a household kerosene lantern was placed in front of metal reflectors or within a glass lens. Toward the end of the nineteenth century, large dioptric lenses manufactures in France or Britain were installed in many lights.

In 1822, French physicist Augustin Fresnel had developed a lens system that revolutionized lighthouse lighting systems around the world. These beehive-shaped assemblies of prisms and lenses were held in place by a metal, usually brass, frame.

Upper and lower prisms directed light to the centre of the lens, where it was magnified by a "bulls-eye" glass at the focal point of the apparatus. The refraction and magnification of the flame (and, later, electric light) at the centre of the lens created a narrow and powerful beam. According to focal distance (the distance between the light source and the bullseye), which ranged from three feet to less than five inches, the lenses were arranged by orders, from first to seventh. First- and second-order lights were commonly found in major landfall lighthouses, while the lower orders guided shipping in and out of smaller harbours and waterways.

The larger lights were rotated on a bath of mercury by a clockwork mechanism, and beginning in the first decade of the twentieth century, many used vapourized kerosene as a light source. Burners ranging in size from twenty-five to eighty-five millimetres used silk mantles to burn the vapourized kerosene, in much the same way that a Coleman lantern operates. By the 1960s most Canadian lighthouses had been converted to electricity. Twenty years later, however, some Scottish lighthouses were still using vapour lamps, and although the systems were out of date, they continued to produce a brilliant light comparable to many electric installations.

Vapour lights required constant attention. Low air pressure or cold vapour tubes (especially during the winter) did not allow the kerosene to vapourise, and the lamp would "flare," causing great amounts of soot to be deposited on the lens and in the lantern. Mary Nickerson, who grew up on Seal Island, west of Cape Sable, remembers that as children she and her brother would sit in a chair and watch the light. If it began to burn irregularly, she would cry "Daddy, the light's flaring" and watch as his storm lantern passed the windows on each level of the light tower as he raced up the stairs to fix the light. He always kept a lantern burning in the house for that reason.

Stations with fog whistles[4] or horns demanded more of the keeper's time. During thick and foggy weather, sound signals were operated to give warning or direction to vessels offshore. Early fog whistles were labour-intensive, and huge amounts of coal and wood were devoured by their hungry boilers. Often boiler tubes blew and belts broke, forcing keepers to shut down machinery and attempt repairs. On smaller stations, bellows-operated hand horns were blown in answer to vessels' calls. In conditions of low visibility, vessels were dependent on guns, whistles, bells and horns until the introduction of radar.

A large part of the keeper's daily routine was taken up with cleaning. Since brass formed a large part of lanterns and lenses, especially toward the turn of the century, much time was spent in polishing. The large dioptric apparatus used in more powerful lights was a marvel of engineering, with its precisely ground prisms and brass frame. Very few of these magnificent lenses remain in the Maritimes; most have been replaced by simple airport-type beacons and compact plastic lenses. Until the introduction of modern lighting systems, keepers maintained a constant level of mercury under the lens by draining and adding the metal depending on the temperature of the air. Engine rooms contained gleaming generators and compressors, and, from the 1920s onward, radio equipment. Most engine rooms were kept spotless by keepers, and one refused to let visitors inside unless they removed their shoes first! In general, the pride of lightkeepers in their work was reflected in their immaculate stations, and this pride was passed from generation to generation.

Canada's lighthouse heyday has come and gone, and today almost all major lights are automated and unattended. Plastic lenses and electric horns are controlled by solid state electronics and remotely monitored over VHF links with central stations. Main lights at major installations flash or turn twenty-four hours a day, and detectors probe the horizon for signs of visibility-reducing fog and vapour to control foghorns. Gone are the days of silently rotating massive lenses, and now the once familiar blast and grunt of the diaphone fog alarm is a fading memory.[5]

The work of the lightkeeper has been taken over by itinerant technicians, mechanics and construction workers who service and maintain station equipment and buildings. Standardized equipment has made most lightstation components interchangeable, with main light and fog signal characteristics determined by electronic circuitry. In the 1980s the Coast Guard began converting minor lights to solar power, reducing the need for regular maintenance at many sites. Fibreglass and open steel towers have replaced many traditional wooden structures. It is doubtful that the lightkeepers of the nineteenth and early twentieth centuries would have been able to comprehend the changes that have occurred on the lights since the days of paraffin vapour and steam horns. In 1992 the families are gone, and only a few lights remain staffed. As the twenty-first century approaches, the importance of lighthouses in practical terms continues to decrease, but they will remain forever an integral part of Maritime history as beacons on welcoming shores.

Coast Guard helicopter at Seal Island. *Chris Mills photo.*

Cross Island light. *Chris Mills photo.*

THREE
Cross Island:
First Light

Although I have explored many lighthouses during my life, it was at Cross Island that I cut my teeth at lightkeeping. Subsequent postings took me to other stations in Nova Scotia and New Brunswick, and although each one had its own character and charm, I have a special attraction to the cluster of white and red buildings on the south point of Cross Island.

It was here that I first experienced the raspy blast of an ice-filled foghorn at four in the morning and the quiet of orange-hued summer evenings. Here I spoke for the first time on a marine VHF radio and learned to survive the tedium of endless days of fog and rain. I walked the shores and revelled in the freedom to plan my day as I wished, and on stormy evenings I came to hear of the spirits which are an integral part of island folklore and Maritime tradition. Most importantly, though, I was thankful that my lifelong dream had been realized; I was at last a lightkeeper, even though it might be only for three weeks!

The weather was blustery as I approached the island in a Canadian Coast Guard helicopter in February. The ride was short; less than ten minutes from Battery Point in Lunenburg. We bumped through rough air above the wooded island as we approached the southern end. The cluster of white buildings and lighthouse was part of the snowscape, set apart only by red roofs and the gleam of the light. After we had touched down, my gear was unloaded on what appeared to be an arctic wasteland. Banks of snow surrounded the buildings and swirls of icy white whipped through the air around the helicopter. George, the departing keeper, unceremoniously piled his gear aboard, and within five minutes the chopper was gone, and with it all traces of mainland civilization. Acting Principal Keeper Ethel Locke helped me unload my supplies into an empty but warm house.

My introduction to Cross Island was different from introductions to other islands in Canada and Great Britain. I had not made a long ferryboat journey or a wave-tossed crossing in a Cape Island fishing boat, nor had I driven on a civilized causeway. I had been dropped out of the air and immediately entered the world of the island only fifteen minutes after I had driven my truck up the road to Battery Point from bustling Lunenburg and the busy highway running by it.

Island life moves at a relaxed pace, regulated by seasons and tides. For the first week of my shift, it was difficult to know exactly how to organize my days. On the mainland, the nine to five, the trips to town, shopping and appointments and the running of a household provide structure for each day. Life on an island lightstation moves slowly. There is rarely any hurry to accomplish chores and work on the grounds, and your work is on the station, not down the street or an hour away in the city.   This was a difficult change to make, and even two years later I would notice the same "adjustment period" on the rotational lightstations.

Cross Island sits at the broad mouth of Lunenburg Harbour, some seven miles south of the busy fishing town. Its 400 acres contain an amazing variety of contrasts: long, sheltered inlets; shale cliffs; quiet woods clearings; a rugged shoreline; grassy bluffs; and winding trails. The island is composed mainly of what is known locally as Feltzen Shale, which lies in east to west ridges. These ridges form several

A young tree swallow held by the author. *E.H. Irwin photo.*

protected fjordlike harbours on the northern end of the island. A road of finely crushed shale runs along the east side, from the north landing to the lightstation. It dips and snakes its way along the shore, past tiny inlets and over shale cliffs. To the west, spruce woods spread over most of the island, interrupted now and then by small clearings and swampy areas.

The island abounds with wildlife. Amidst the raucous cries of Herring and Great Blackbacked gulls, deer browse along the shore and muskrats swim in the still ponds, disappearing with a splash at the sight and sound of humans. Small birds fill the spruce woods, and mice and voles populate the grassy banks. The island is home to a variety of sparrows, crossbills, finches and a healthy population of grass snakes. In the summer one sees serpents of all sizes on the lightstation lawn, under old boards and along the dusty road. One relief lightkeeper who was terrified of the limbless reptiles refused to stay on the island, and the lightstation logbook recorded that he had departed the lighthouse, "unable to cope with island life."

During the spring, the grassy banks and bluffs along the shore come alive with hundreds of wheeling, protective gulls. Along the banks and hollows, most nests hold three brown speckled eggs which will in a short time become speckled gull chicks. Ducks and sandpipers also nest on the island and add to the general mayhem when disturbed by lightkeepers and visitors on foot.

In the quiet of early morning and evening, the deer will come to the lighthouse to feed on the short and tender grass of the lawn. Once I climbed the tower at dusk to watch three deer in the field behind the station. As I stood on the lantern deck, I thought of the recent morning when I had risen at 0300 hours to check the weather. The fog was thick, and as I opened the door I was startled by a form silhouetted by the outside light on the engine room. It was a deer, feeding, apparently unconcerned by my presence. I went quickly back inside, but my scent must have reached him, for he sniffed once and then shot along the southern shore as the horn sent two hoarse blasts into the fog.

Cross Island is a ghost settlement, where weathered fish stores and piles of slowly rotting timbers are the only reminders of a once bustling fishing community. Apple trees and garden bushes surround crumbling foundations and piles of weathered board that were once houses and sheds. Narrow paths beaten in the long grass by summer visitors wind through the settlement on the island's main harbour, and a larger trail circles the southern and western shores, leading to the lighthouse.

Sixteen fishermen and their families once lived on the island, mostly on the north side of the harbour,[6] from where they went handlining for cod, herring, mackerel and haddock. Before the development of marine gasoline engines, small sailing vessels worked the fishing grounds. Partly as a result of the increased use of the internal combustion engine in fishing boats, and partly through the lure of mainland amenities, the island lost its resident population in the first two decades of the

Old Levy house, 1989. *Chris Mills photo.*

twentieth century. Those who left continued to fish from mainland communities. On the island, their abandoned homes and stores have since rotted, and today only the Levy house and one original shed remain standing.

According to one account, Portuguese interests may have brought the sixteenth-century explorer Joao Alvares Fagundez to the island of "San Francisco" off the coast of Nova Scotia — possibly Cross Island. Although there is no evidence of Portuguese settlement, the island did have a permanent population of fishing families by the mid-eighteenth century. In 1752 the island was granted to one Edmund Crawley, member of an early Halifax naval family, by Governor Cornwallis.[7] A Randall S. Crawley settled on the island around this time; it is probable that he was related to Edmund. A 1752 census recorded that Cross Island was inhabited by thirty-six males and one female over the age of sixteen, and one male under the age of sixteen.[8] More than 100 years later, the population of the island had diminished to sixteen. By this time, six oxen, four cows, three swine and seventy sheep competed for territory with the human residents.

A map drawn by the Reverend H.L. Owen in 1869 noted that robins were seen on the island all year long and that crows from the mainland sheltered there in the evenings while wild fowl gathered by day. One hundred and twenty years later I observed crows flocking over the trees west of the lighthouse on most evenings, settling for the night. Eider ducks, commonly known as "sea ducks," continue to nest and feed around the island. Notes on the crude map also identified several types of wood found on Cross Island's 400 acres, including spruce, hackmatack, ironwood, birch, fir, maple, dogwood, alder and hemlock.[9] Today, spruce appears to be predominant, although some deciduous growth occurs around the old settlement and throughout the interior of the island. During his time on the island, George Locke found only one maple tree, on the west point of the island.

The original settlers cleared some land and grew crops for food and raised sheep and a few cows. Until recently, lightkeepers on the island supplemented their incomes by fishing and kept vegetable gardens. Today the remains of several garden plots can be seen around the station, in the woods and near the remnants of the wharf built by George at the northern end of the lighthouse road.

Cross Island has also been called Prince of Wales Island and Cunningham's Island. When a lighthouse was erected in 1834, a large black cross was painted on the side of the structure for use as a daymark and to distinguish it from the lights at Sambro and Liverpool. It has been suggested that the island received its present name from this symbol on the tower. Another theory is that the island was named for a large wooden cross which may have been erected on the southern end of the island for navigational purposes by French explorers.[10]

During the latter part of the 1820s, merchants, shipowners and fishing interests in Lunenburg town and county petitioned the government for the erection of a lighthouse for the benefit of local and colonial trade.[11] Concerns were voiced for the safety of vessels caught in bad weather, and about the difficulty they would have in making Lunenburg Harbour without a guiding light on Cross Island. The establishment of this light would complete the chain of lights from Sambro to Cape Sable and consequently afford safe passage for vessels up and down the south coast of the province.

On December 26, 1834, notice was given in *The Novascotian* that: "A Light house has ... been erected on Cross Island, near Lunenburg Harbour — the tower is white and it is intended to paint on it a strong black cross 5 feet wide, to designate it from Sambro or Liverpool in day time; it is not yet lighted — when the mode of lighting is determined, a further notice with a more minute description of its bearings &c will be given."[12]

The good merchants and citizens of Lunenburg were not entirely satisfied with the service they received, as further notice of the station's "mode of lighting" did not come for another five years! By 1835 the lighthouse and keeper's house had been painted red to make them more identifiable from sea, and finally on the first of December 1839[13] the light was lit, no doubt to the great relief of the local population. Since that night the light on Cross Island has been sustained by whale, seal and porpoise oils, kerosene and electricity. Today's light is a ten-inch rotating airport-type beacon which turns twenty-four hours a day, powered by electricity from the mainland.

The original tower and several other buildings burned in 1960 when an oil furnace caused a fire in the adjacent engine room. The replacement tower was a functional steel structure which was in turn replaced two decades later by a fibreglass tower. Although modern in design, today's version resembles an archetypal lighthouse more than its predecessor. Today it stands between the vacant keepers' houses, padlocked, and monitored from Ketch Harbour, fifty-five kilometres distant.

As early as 1827, one Robert Stone had petitioned the government to be appointed "superintendent" of the lighthouse, but it was not until 1835 that a keeper was hired. He was Jacob Smith, originally from Liverpool, England. During the War of 1812, Smith had been press-ganged and put aboard a British warship. When the vessel called at Halifax, Jacob jumped ship and made his way to Sambro where he lived for a time before marrying a Lunenburg County woman, Sophia Rhost. Together they settled on Cross Island, raising five children while Jacob fished.[14] Jacob served as the keeper of the light for more than thirty years; in the late 1860s he was succeeded by his son Edward. In the mid-1870s Edward's son continued the tradition, working as assistant keeper. Almost a century later, great grandson Earl "Smitty" Smith became a keeper, serving twenty-one years on the island until his retirement in 1980. Earl left the island upon finishing his time as a keeper, but returned to his summer camp every year until his death in 1991. In 1981 George Locke assumed the position of head keeper and eight years later was the last senior lightkeeper in the station's 155-year history.

Most lighthouse work is basic: mowing, painting, cleaning. On fine days, part of the day is spent painting the shed that couldn't be done last week because of rain, and filling in potholes in the road. We work eight-hour shifts, from 0200 to 1000 and 1400 to 2200. On Saturdays we change shifts to alter the procedure a little. Undeniably, routine is one of the aspects of lightkeeping that has not changed since the beginning. Twice-daily radio schedules and a variety of domestic chores provide the framework upon which lighthouse life is based. Work is usually conducted at a steady pace so everything is not done at once and there is something left to do tomorrow.

On days that dawned clear, I began my chores after breakfast — cleaning the fog detector lenses, washing down the engine room floor, replacing flourescent lights, scrubbing down the lantern room and washing salt off lantern windows. There were furnace oil tanks to fill and the station lawn to mow. The industrial mowers we used had seen better days and it was not uncommon to see them dismantled on the garage floor while we sharpened the blades and cursed the carburetors. Nevertheless, all of these tasks were enjoyable, as the end result was a tidy and well maintained station.

Many of my journal entries from this period record the routine tasks that made up so many days; others relate experiences that struck me as important at the time. Here's an entry written one calm summer evening:

Where else can you sit on your back step — have a sip of rum and coke and take in the vista — the placid evening sea and sky, the gulls wheeling around the southwest point and the sun setting slowly over the island. In the distance, West Ironbound lies like an enchanted isle, its cliffs shrouded in the low evening mist. Soon its yellow light will begin to blink, every 10 seconds. Next door to my own house, our light's rays will sweep over the waters and the field. As darkness falls the crows will begin their nightly ritual, circling noisily over the trees before settling in for the night. I run the tractor to the north wharf and take the skiff to the slipway where I haul it up to take a walk through the long grass and spruce trees. In the distance I hear the horn start up as the first wisps of fog wrap the trees. I head back to the wharf, navigating the boat through the still and silent fog shrouded inlets and walk back along the quiet lighthouse road.

I spent many evenings walking around the station, enjoying the smells and sights. With a garden chair and a book at the edge of the lawn, I could read until dark amidst the salt air and soft breezes. At dusk I watched the rhythmic flash of the Tanner Island light to the northeast and found comfort in its regularity. Late afternoon walks along the lighthouse road held the promise of smells of spruce and salt, and the sight of deer browsing kelp on the shore. The whole scene was so relaxing and peaceful at times that it was difficult to believe that there were any problems in the outside world, if indeed the outside world existed at all.

Nonetheless, things weren't always so tranquil. In the winter, easterly gales whipped up the surf until the coves along the light road were filled with six feet of salty foam. It was often difficult to quietly reflect and think profound thoughts while a forty-knot gale was blowing sleet and rain across my face like salt from a blunderbuss. There were also seemingly endless days of fog in the summer when the constant blare of the horn and the drip, drip of water into the cistern in my basement from fog-sodden eaves became as surely maddening as a Chinese water torture.

Outsiders often view the life of a lightkeeper as being a pleasantly contemplative one, and although this sounds good in theory, it does not always hold true. After several weeks of isolation, especially during periods of bad weather, the contemplation of philosophy and nature can turn to the less intellectual study of one's navel. The lack of social contact can create a feeling of malaise that is hard to break. Interestingly enough, though, I was never really lonely on Cross Island or any of the later lights. If I ever did feel alone, it was never as a

Winter sunset. *Chris Mills photo.*

An evening shift in winter, Cross Island. *Chris Mills photo.*

One of the north end "fjords" on Cross Island. *Chris Mills photo.*

Author working on journals, Cross Island. *Chris Mills photo.*

result of being physically isolated. I think the hardest part for me was having too much time to think and not enough to do in running the station. Nonetheless, when the sun broke out and the skies cleared, it was as if all bad thoughts and feelings had been banished and I could once again roam the shores and woods with a clear head.

Although sometimes it seemed as though the possibility of fog was never far off, summer days on the island were often clear and hot. Around the harbour and through the woods, the conditions seemed arid despite the closeness of the surrounding ocean:

> The lighthouse road is dry and dusty; grasshoppers leave little explosions of grey in the shale as they jump. Although the heat of the day lingers throughout the afternoon on the northern end of the island, the air gets cooler as one gets closer to the lightstation on the southern point. As you climb the final hills before reaching the open fields around the lighthouse the wind begins to ruffle your hair. And then, unbelievably, it is cold and windy and the horn starts to blow. Through the heat of the day a bank of fog has been lurking on the horizon, waiting to move in. When it moves, it does so with amazing speed. Almost immediately the mood of the island changes. With the wisps of a wet fog swirling above in the light, the whole world reduces to the lightstation. Anything outside the lighthouse compound does not exist. When the fog lifts, maybe a few hours later, maybe a few weeks later, a larger world of trees, fields, water, distant islands and the mainland once again becomes reality.

Occasionally a small plane would circle the station and drop newspapers to the keepers. The pilot was a dentist friend of the Lockes from Mahone Bay. He was a good shot and was able to hit the top of my house with one delivery. Another time George and I had been walking around the island and were spotted by the plane while we were near the north wharf. Once again the pilot's aim was good: the packet landed less than twenty feet from where we were standing. It was always enjoyable to read the papers, even though we had TV and radio. The newspaper is in some ways a more immediate form of journalism than radio or TV because it is held and read, and thus a more interactive way of being informed. Although TV reception was good on the island I watched very little, being more content outside, working around the station or walking around the island. The radio was a constant companion though, especially during the days of wind, rain, sleet and snow.

In the summer the waters around the island are filled with all manner of boats: yachts, speedboats, fishing vessels, naval ships. The *Bluenose II* passed by the lightstation on a couple of occasions, and a gaff-rigged schooner beating against the wind to reach Lunenburg was a fairly common sight and brought to mind how the harbour approaches must have appeared a century earlier. Old petitions for the construction of the lighthouse said Lunenburg ranked second among the ports of the province, based on the amount of duties paid into the treasury; the waters would have been filled with coastal schooners and larger cargo vessels. During the first three decades of the twentieth century, a large fleet of Grand Banks schooners regularly passed Cross Island on their way to and from the rich fishing grounds off Newfoundland. Today a fleet of thirty-five to forty modern draggers and two freezer-trawlers sets sail from the port, travelling to the offshore fishing grounds on the Grand, Brown's and George's banks and up to Greenland for cod.

Summer is a busy time on the island, with a constant stream of visitors. The arrival of the first summer people in June heralds the beginning of the social year on Cross Island, when regulars and tourists motor and sail to the island to enjoy the quiet and the heat. Generations of Spindlers, Levys, Smiths and DeMones have visited the island, relaxing aboard boats and walking through the woods and along the shorelines. In the short time I spent on Cross Island I can remember many evenings sitting in the hot, crowded cabins of converted Cape Island fishing boats, sipping rum, telling tales and listening to Newfoundland music from the local radio station.

During my last night on the station, with my gear packed and ready for my final trip ashore the next day, I had reflected on island life and the culture of the people who had for so many years formed these close, isolated communities. Traditions and stories were passed from generation to generation until they became part of the very fabric of island life. Before radio and, especially, television introduced passive forms of entertainment, singing and storytelling were common forms of amusement and were also methods of preserving and perpetuating the island people's sense of identity.

Most islands have ghost tales of shipwrecked sailors, drowned fishermen and old lightkeepers. As mentioned before, Canada's oldest existing lighthouse is said to be haunted by the ghost of Alex Alexander, a young soldier who hung himself or was murdered on the island more than a century ago. Until the removal of the keepers from Sambro Island in 1988, Double Alex made his presence known on several occasions, including one night when he reportedly attempted to climb into bed with a young female guest.

One evening as keeper John Fairservice was returning to the island in the station boat, he saw a figure walking along the nearby beach. Assuming that it was the assistant keeper, John became annoyed when the man did not come down to help haul up the boat. Later he learned that at the time he had seen the figure, his assistant had been in bed, fast asleep. But there were only the two men on the island, so the identity of the figure on the beach remains a mystery to this day.

Eighteen kilometres to the northeast, Devil's Island is also said to be haunted. Although the lightkeepers have been gone for a quarter of a century, visitors and spirit-seekers have reported strange occurrences on the island in recent years. In the fall of 1990, Rip Irwin spent three nights on the island

Northern shore, Cross Island. *Chris Mills photo.*

during his travels to Eastern Shore lighthouses. A few days before his arrival, vandals had landed on the island, breaking into the lighthouse and the deserted keeper's house. Rip found an old piece of iron from the remains of the original lighthouse lantern and used it to secure the door on the house, which had been left open.

Close to midnight on a moonless night, he was startled to see a dull glow in one of the first floor windows of the deserted lightkeeper's house. The light continued to burn as he approached the house, and then suddenly went out, as if a candle had been snuffed. With no moon and no lights on the nearby shore it couldn't have been a reflection, he thought, as he entered the dwelling, and the door had been wedged shut with the piece of iron. Inside it was quiet and dark. On the kitchen table was a candle and he fancied that the wax near the wick was slightly warm and that the lingering smell of burned wick hung in the air, but he couldn't be sure. There was no one else on the island.

During fourteen years as lightkeepers, George and Ethel Locke experienced their fair share of strange occurrences. Before moving to Cross Island in 1981, they served on three other lightstations along the Eastern Shore and in Cape Breton. In the late 1970s, George, Ethel, Daniel, Denise and Sandra lived on Country Island in Guysborough County. Soon after their arrival, footfalls in the basement and up through the house awakened family members, as did the crashing sound of pipes being dropped on a cement floor. In both cases George found nothing disturbed and the basement door closed and latched from the inside.

There was a presence on Country Island. The children felt it, even during daylight hours, and they refused to play outside after supper. On the other islands they had all spent their evenings outside, especially in nice weather. Country Island was different though. "Oh no, Daddy," they said, "there's something watching us." George felt it too as he made his rounds of the station and as he walked down the boardwalk to

George and Ethel Locke, 1990. *Chris Mills photo.*

the engine room in the early morning. He said it almost seemed as though someone was walking behind him, but at the same time the sensation did not come from any particular direction.

The Locke's chihuahua sensed something as well. He would suddenly stop in his tracks, raising his hackles and growling at the invisible presence. When the Locke children spent evenings with the Head Keeper and his wife in their house next to their own, they would wait for their father to come and walk them home, even though the two houses on the station were only a short distance apart. No one seemed to know who or what was watching, but the presence had been on the island for some time. The head keeper had worked on the island in the 1940s and had witnessed some strange events himself during that time.

Years before, the lightkeeper's young son, infected with tuberculosis, had lived on the island. In order to isolate him, the boy was placed in a building separate from the lighthouse. The story goes that he was fed his meals on the step of the lighthouse and once bled from the mouth onto the doorstep. It was said that until the demolition of the structure in 1968 the blood stain could not be washed off or covered by paint. The lad eventually died, but not on the island.

On nearby Goose Island the ghosts of French soldiers who perished in a shipwreck two centuries ago were seen by Country's lightkeepers and local residents. Although the Lockes weren't ever able to explain their experiences on Country Island, they realized that they were not the only people to have witnessed strange happenings on the isle of spirits.

On Cross Island the spirits made an appearance within a couple of years of the Lockes' arrival. At dusk one evening, young Daniel took the tractor back along the lighthouse road after leaving his father at the north side. George and a friend of the family had gone to check on one of the summer homes when they thought they saw a light in a window across the harbour. Halfway along the road, near a small harbour called Oil Cove, Daniel saw a shadowy figure standing in the middle of the lane. Startled, he sped the tractor up and drove through the figure. When he stopped and turned around there was no one in sight.

George later said that Daniel "hollered so loud we could hear him from the north end of the island!" The figure had been wearing a roll-neck sweater, like fishermen used to wear and had a long-bearded face. Despite muddy conditions, no footprints or other evidence that someone had stood in the road could be found, and there was no one else on the island. After this encounter Daniel refused to walk or drive along the light road after dark. Later, Earl Smith told them that the old man's name was Whynacht and that he had been a lightkeeper on the island many years ago. Daniel's description of the bearded figure fit the old keeper's appearance exactly.

On two occasions Ethel had experiences that gave her cause to wonder. One morning she watched a small open boat come through the narrow north entrance to the harbour (the "gut") as she stood on the wharf. It entered the harbour and passed by the moored lightstation boat, where George and Daniel were working. She saw a man standing at the tiller of the craft and assumed that it was Earl Smith, who often came to the island to spend time at his fish store. She heard the boat's engine, and although it sounded a little different from the usual outboard, she didn't take much notice of it at the time. Later, she asked George if he had spoken to Earl, and was surprised to find that he and Daniel had seen and heard nothing. She was crazy, he said, there had been no boat.

On the next occasion, Ethel was once again on the wharf while George and Daniel were at the government slipway, on the northern end of the island, painting the station boat. She saw a small open boat come through the gut as before and again assumed that it was Earl Smith. She saw the boat close by to the station boat and thought Earl was talking with Daniel and George, and then she watched it pass through the eastern entrance to the harbour and out of sight.

When Daniel came to the wharf to bring her to the slipway, she asked him how Earl was. Daniel looked at her strangely and said they hadn't seen anyone. But she had, she said. Hadn't they seen anything? By this time everyone was wondering if Ethel was seeing things, so when Earl and his wife Rita were visiting the Lockes at the lightstation some time later, Ethel asked Earl if he had been around the harbour in his boat. He replied that he hadn't even been near the island at the time and then asked her to describe the boat she had seen. When she did, he turned white. He told her that she had seen Jim Burgoyne, a fisherman who had been drowned on the Shaving Mill Ledges off the western side of the island several decades ago. Jim had lived on the island, above his fish store (now used by Bobby Spindler as a summer camp). After this startling revelation, Ethel realized that there had been something different about the boat. It was the sound it had made as it had passed through the harbour — not the steady growl of a modern diesel or the roar of an outboard, but a "putt putt" that identified it as an old gas engine, a "make and break." Her voice would crack when she told the story. Make and breaks hadn't been used by fishermen for decades.

These stories were all the more poignant as I sat in the Lockes' bright kitchen, with a gale force wind howling around the house, and the foghorn sending its throaty rasp into the murk. Times had changed on Cross Island in the eight years since the five Lockes had arrived to take care of the lighthouse. In the beginning they had formed a little community, along with the assistant keeper's family on the southern end of the island. In the summer there were vegetable gardens to be tended, fish to be caught and outdoor activities of all sorts for the lightstation kids. As the Locke children grew and moved off the island to work and raise families of their own, Ethel worked as assistant keeper for six months at a stretch, alternating with other term employees to fill the junior position. With the children gone and the second dwelling empty for six months of the year, George and Ethel were the only inhabitants of the island for much of the year. Although summer brought activity to the north harbour and visitors to the lightstation, the atmosphere of the place had changed.

When I arrived on the island I knew that things were drawing to a close. One year earlier, Coast Guard officials had met with fishermen and boaters in Lunenburg to discuss plans to destaff the lighthouse. Although there was opposition to the idea, the Coast Guard decided that by the fall of 1989 the station would be fully automated and the keepers removed.

During the early part of the summer we learned that the lighthouse would be destaffed in July instead of the autumn as had been originally planned. Although I knew this had been a possibility all along, the news came as a shock. I had hoped to spend six months on the station, the maximum time allowable for a casual employee. We prepared to leave the island, spending the weeks prior to July 10 packing up the contents of George's house and moving deckloads of belongings ashore in the station boat.

On the morning of the tenth, thick fog moved in, delaying the arrival of the helicopter and the workmen who would close up the station, so George and I returned to shore on the lightstation boat. At the Lockes' home in Feltzen there was a great deal of activity while preparations were made for moving. A crew from CBC television had arrived, and when we returned to the island, George was interviewed for a local news feature and for CBC Midday. It was an emotional time for George, especially. He had spent eight years on the station with his family and had been content in being his own supervisor on the wooded isle. Although he had known for some time that he would have to leave the island for good in the not too distant future, it was difficult to see everything packed up and removed from his family's home of eight years.

The telephone connection was made on the lighthouse VHF, and while the camera and microphones were set up, the Toronto producer made helpful suggestions. Hastily passing the VHF microphone to the interviewer, I stepped aside to watch the proceedings, while in the background, work crews emptied our houses and packed up furniture. As the videotape rolled, I stood out of the camera's view, blocking wind from the microphone while George attempted to sum up his feelings towards lightkeeping for thousands of Canadians sitting in front of their televisions. Although the interview was not difficult for George, the final look through his house of eight years was. Somehow the camera didn't (or couldn't) quite capture the sadness of departure, I thought, as I watched news footage of the lightstation a few nights later.

Later that day the chopper slung the remainder of the Lockes' belongings ashore and took the rest of us off for the last time. A Coast Guard crew removed fridges and freezers from the island and began to board up dwellings. One hundred fifty-five years of lightkeeping on Cross Island had come to an unceremonious end. Now, with the Lockes gone, the restless spirits are left to patrol the quiet woods and trails and abandoned sheds, disturbed only in the summer by those who return to renew their acquaintance with the island.

Left: Acting Head Keeper Glenn McCabe on lantern deck. Right: Removing the keeper's belongings, 1989. *Chris Mills photos.*

Wreck of the *Fermont*, Seal Island. *Chris Mills photo.*

FOUR
Seal Island:
Seals, Shipwrecks & Sheep

If I had another life to live I would want to spend every
minute of it here on Seal Island.

Winifred Hamilton, from *Yarmouth Vanguard* article
Wednesday, Feb. 10, 1982, "Winifred Hamilton, the
dame of Seal Island, remembered."
by Genevieve MacCrae

SEAL ISLAND ranks with other graveyards of the Atlantic —
Saint Paul's, Scatarie and Sable islands — as a seducer of ships
and a claimant of lives. From Clark's Harbour on Cape Sable
Island the island is invisible by day, but as dusk falls, its
powerful light can be seen sweeping the horizon at ten-second
intervals. Lying roughly eighteen nautical miles due west of the
tallest lighthouse in Nova Scotia at Cape Sable, Seal Island is
by day and night a traffic sign for fishing boats, pleasure craft
and commercial cargo ships travelling the sea road to the Bay
of Fundy and the eastern seaboard of the United States.

Roughly three miles long from north to south, one mile
wide and composed of granite and glacial till, it is the largest of
the five islands in the vicinity. Seal, Mud, Flat, Round and
Noddy islands are an extension of the Tuskets, which run
southward from Wedgeport on the Nova Scotia mainland.
They are collectively known as the Seal Islands, or "Iles aux
Loups Marins," as they were named by explorer Samuel de

Champlain in 1604. For more than three centuries these islands have witnessed both the safe and tragic passage of vessels navigating the fog- and storm-bound waters of southwestern Nova Scotia.

Seal Island's history is remarkable, not only because a huge number of ships have been lost on its shore and surrounding ledges, but as a reflection of the diligence and tenacity of the people who first settled there to patrol the shoreline and give assistance to shipwrecked mariners. One hundred sixty-nine years after the first settlement of the east and west sides, descendants of the Hichens and Crowells continue to travel to the island in the spring, living on the east side until autumn gives way to winter's gales. The last lightkeeper on the island in 1990 was the husband of Mary Nickerson, the great grand-niece of Mary Hichens, Canada's own lighthouse heroine. It was mainly through Mrs. Hichens' efforts that the two families moved to the island in 1823 to assist mariners cast up on the island's inhospitable shores.

Mary Hichens' work is representative of the services performed by countless lighthouse women alongside their male counterparts. Women have played a key role in the operation of lighthouses in Canada and around the world since the first lights shone out over the water. Although well known lighthouse heroines such as Grace Darling of the Longstone Light in England, and Ida Lewis of Lime Rock in Rhode Island[15] accomplished great acts of daring and heroism, there have been many others who spent hours and days tending seal oil and kerosene lights alongside their husbands and families. In some cases the women carried on lightkeeping duties after their husbands died, often until their own retirements. In Cape Breton, Eliza Campbell brought up three children and kept the west light on Scatarie Island for twenty-one years after the drowning death of her husband in 1942. In 1975 Marjorie Fairservice obtained the position of assistant keeper on Sambro Island alongside her husband, who had been a keeper

The lighthouse with visitors. *Chris Mills photo.*

since 1964. On many other stations, wives took the places of vacationing keepers, in some cases receiving no remuneration for their work.

Like most lighthouse women, Mary Hichens' contributions to lifesaving are not well known, but long before Grace or Ida rowed to the rescue of shipwrecked mariners, Mary's dream of lifesaving services and a lighthouse on Seal Island had become a reality. The result of her desire and dedication continues to operate 161 years after it was first lighted and continues to perform the same task, guiding vessels around the island and warning of the outlying reefs and shoals.

Mary was the daughter of Barrington preacher Thomas Crowell. She was descended from *Mayflower* and New England Puritan stock and perhaps as a result of this background was the kind of person to feel duty bound to assist the unfortunate souls cast ashore on Seal Island. No doubt she had been deeply affected by the stories of sailors wrecked there, and when Richard Hichens came into her life, her desire to aid them gained direction.

Richard had been born at Penzance in Cornwall and, after serving during the Napoleonic Wars, he sailed to Halifax as the master of a brig. In December 1816 he left the port of Castries in St. Lucia with a cargo of sugar on the brig *Friendship*, bound for Halifax. During the early part of January 1817, the brig sighted Cape Sable, much to the relief of Captain and crew. The voyage had been arduous. They had weathered several storms and the deaths of several crewmembers had left the vessel shorthanded. As they approached Cape Sable, a freezing gale buffeted the ship, coating it with ice. Trapped in the ledges around the Cape, the vessel lost its rudder. The crew managed to make shore, landing on the uninhabited sand island (it would be another forty-four years before a lighthouse was built on Cape Sable). Sheltering themselves in holes they dug in the sand, their ship was eventually spotted by residents of nearby Cape Sable Island.

Hichens and his crewmembers were cared for in Cape

The *Fermont* was run aground on Seal Island in 1991, where its massive hull remains today. *Chris Mills photo.*

Triumph graves near Mother Owens Point, Seal Island. *Chris Mills photo.*

Island homes, and when the captain travelled to Barrington to enter his account of the wreck with the notary public, he was taken in by Thomas Crowell, known locally as "Uncle Tommy." Richard fell in love with Mary, the young daughter of Tommy Crowell, and they were soon married. Along with another couple, Edmund and Jerusha Crowell, the Hichens settled on Seal Island, building homesteads on the east and west sides of the island. A candle burned in the window of each house, assuring each family by night that all was well with the other, and guiding any unfortunate sailors cast ashore.

Around the island, Blonde Rock, Devil's Limb, Limb's Limb and Mother Owen's Rock have been the killers of many a wooden-hulled ship's crew. The number of shipwrecks there is impressive, considering that much of what is now the Atlantic Provinces was not settled for a century after the first wrecks on the island. According to Winifred Hamilton, one of the first shipwrecks occurred almost 150 years prior to the arrival of the first families on Seal Island in 1823: on August 25, 1676, the captain of a brig from New Haven, Connecticut, and his crew of two struggled ashore on the uninhabited isle. Within three weeks the two crewmembers had died, only days before the captain was rescued by a passing vessel.

Since that time at least 160 vessels have been stranded or wrecked around the island, including seventeen caught in the clutches of the notorious Blonde Rock, three and a half miles south of Mother Owens Rock. This tide-washed ledge was named after HMS *Blonde*, a warship used against New England privateers. In the spring of 1782 the *Blonde* overtook the *Lyon* of Massachusetts and set off for Halifax with the captured crew aboard. In thick fog the vessel struck the rock which now bears its name; the crew and prisoners made Seal Island with some provisions but were marooned by fog for several days.

Ironically, they were rescued by two American privateers who set the British ship's crew on the mainland in exchange for the crew of the *Lyon*. Before removing all the men from the island, the captain ordered the crew of the *Blonde* to get rid of their weapons. They did so, throwing pistols and muskets into a small deep pond above the shingle beach on the east side of the island. "Brig Pond" remains to this day, although its size and depth have changed over the years as storms have pushed the beach further inland. In recent years no evidence of the jettisoned weapons has been found.

Throughout the first half of the twentieth century, ships and fishing vessels continued to come to grief in the waters surrounding Seal Island, and occasionally today the skeleton timbers of wrecks show above the shifting sands of the east beach. In 1944 the sixty-six-ton *Elk* of Gloucester, Massachusetts, went aground on the east side in a thick fog and the ship's rusting engine is still visible at low tide. In November 1991 the freighter *Fermont* became the island's latest wreck when it was run aground between Little Head Yard and Head Yard on the eastern side of the island. Ironically, it came ashore thirteen months after the last keepers left the lighthouse. Stripped of its engines and salvageable equipment, it has been left to disintegrate amongst the moving sands of the long beach.

Many sailors lucky enough to survive the breaking-up of their vessels were not so fortunate when they reached the shores of the desolate, wind-blown island. There was little shelter or warmth to be found amongst the stunted spruce trees or along the dirt embankments, and many sailors perished on the beaches. One man was found frozen to death, crouched over a small pile of sticks he had vainly attempted to light with flint and steel.

Each spring, preachers and residents from Yarmouth and Barrington would come to the island to bury the bodies washed up along its inhospitable shores. Stories of the preachers' grim spring task reached the mainland, causing many people to speak of the need for a lifesaving station or lighthouse on the island. For some time there had been local interest in a permanent settlement of "people of good character" to fish from the island and give assistance to shipwrecked mariners,

Seal Island Church, 1984. *Chris Mills photo.*

and finally in 1823 this interest was realized.

After the arrival of the Hichens and Crowells, the value of a human presence on Seal Island was soon made evident. During the winter of 1827, the ship *Vivid* ran aground on Race Point in a fierce snowstorm. Although the crewmembers were able to safely reach shore by dropping off the end of the jib boom onto the rocks, they faced bleak prospects for survival on what seemed to be an uninhabited island. A party of the frozen and exhausted men discovered a trail through the woods and stumbled along it until, unbelievably, they saw a light shining in the distance. The men reached Edmund Crowell's house guided by the candle in the window and, not long after, the remainder of the crew was led through the woods to safety.

It soon became apparent that more than lifesaving services would be required to lessen the dangers to ships passing by Seal Island. In 1827 Lieutenant-Governor James Kempt visited the island and, after seeing the island and the record of shipwrecks kept by the Hichens, agreed that a lighthouse would much reduce the number of ships lost there. The commissioner of lighthouses, Samuel Cunard, with his vested interest in shipping, also saw the great need to mark the island with a light,[16] and so in 1830 the construction of a large wooden-beamed structure began.

On November 28, 1831, the Seal Island lighthouse sent its first rays into the darkness; and on the very same night a daughter Sarah was born to Richard and Mary Hichens. The lighthouse tower was constructed of massive timbers and beams, and braced with heavy cross members and natural-growth knees. The original octagonal structure remains in use today, although the sheathing and shingling have been renewed twice. In 1978, the 1902 vintage lantern and classical lens were removed and replaced with a functional modern lantern and a rotating airport-type beacon. Through the work of local residents and the Barrington Historical Society, the light apparatus and lantern were moved ashore and installed as the centrepiece of the Seal Island Light Museum in Barrington.

Between 1831 and 1927 the light was maintained by the Hichens-Crowell family and their descendants. Initially Richard Hichens and Edmund Crowell kept the light, each working six months at a time at the station. In 1855, Edmund's son Corning took over duties at the light, and eventually Corning Junior became keeper. When he died in 1891, his brother John took over. Upon John Crowell's death in 1927, Ellsworth Hamilton became keeper. Ellsworth's wife was John's daughter Winifred; after her husband died in 1941 she remained on the island for another forty-one years until her own death at the age of ninety-three.

In 1941, though, with the war in full swing, the light was

about to pass out of Crowell hands altogether. The Hamilton's son Max was a few months too young to be eligible for the position, and it was imperative that the vacancy be filled immediately. Between 1939 and 1944 lightkeepers on both the Atlantic and Pacific coasts played a crucial role in coastal defense. At regular intervals throughout the day, designated stations listened for radio instructions regarding the operation of navigational equipment — lights, horns and radiobeacons — that would be as useful to enemy vessels and aircraft as they were to friendly coastal traffic. Keepers were instructed to report immediately any sightings of enemy craft, and several lightstations became official observation posts for the Detection Corps of the Royal Canadian Air Force. With Max a few months short of his twenty-first birthday, Winifred hoped that the position would stay open until he was old enough to take it. But this was not to be. Lewis Spinney was to become the seventh principal lightkeeper to take charge of the station.

So, in 1941, for the first time in 110 years, the care of the Seal Island light passed entirely out of the hands of the Crowell family. Between 1941 and 1990, ten principal keepers and countless assistants worked on the station, the last being (acting) Principal Keeper Brian Stoddard, who left the island on October 16, 1990, one day before the light was fully automated.

My own experience of Seal Island spans two decades, and although I have no blood ties to the place, I have a strong attachment to its shores, woods and lighthouse. I was seven when I first saw the island from the deck of a rolling Cape Island fishing boat. My parents' birdwatching trips brought us to the island once or twice a year until we children had grown and gone abroad to work and study. For fifteen years though, along with good friends, the McLarens, we spent summer and autumn holidays exploring the island, prowling through the woods and clambering over the boulder-strewn beaches. I grew to love the isle and can remember countless times when I prayed that the weather would be too rough for the boat to come and get us. I recall submitting notes from my parents explaining my absence from school while we watched huge waves smash the west-side wharf. And I remember being quietly proud as the teacher asked "Where was it that you spent your holidays ... on an island *how* far from the mainland?"

My earliest memories of the island are a mixture of sights and smells. There were the rugged weathered shacks on the east and west sides, wide slipways, the old cracked cement wharf, the white rectangle of the North Home, quite mossy woods, the broad sand beach backed by rippling dunes, the activitity of fishermen and mossers, the long, winding sheltered road to the lighthouse, the steady roar of the lightstation generators, the moan of the foghorn on foggy, damp and drippy days and the distant roar of the surf from my creaky rope bunk in the North Home attic. In 1990 I renewed my acquaintance with these places and with the smells I had come to associate with the island over the years. In my lighthouse journal I noted:

> The smells of Seal Island are essential to its character. The tang of drying Irish Moss on the sheep cropped grass of the East Side, and the pungent odour of kelp lying in huge rolls on the shingle beach as the swell washes it clean. Fields of purple flags and their spicy aroma, musky smell of sheep, salty tang of seaweed and driftwood and the sun-baked beach stone. The rich smell of decaying kelp and seaweed in Saltwater Pond, the tidal flat south east of the East Side church, the smell of paint and diesel on the lightstation, and the glorious scent of evening — a soft breeze carrying combined essences of tide, shore and woods.

We stayed mainly in the North Home, one of the remaining buildings in the small settlement across the cove from the west side. It had been used for years by fishermen

Sheep roam wild on the west side of the island. *Chris Mills photo.*

Troll Camp, 1988. *Mary McLaren photo.*

during the lobster season. Around 1970 it was purchased by several members of the Nova Scotia Bird Society, to be used as a base for birdwatching expeditions. An austere dwelling with four rooms and a lean-to entrance, it "boasts one of the most derelict and best ventilated outhouses in Atlantic Canada." As children our trips to answer nature's call at three in the morning were as expeditious as possible. Who knew what dangers lurked below the dark and drafty hole in the seat?

In the house, the downstairs kitchen is dominated by a large chrome and green enamel Lady Scotia woodstove, and behind it two doorways lead to a small pantry and a tiny bedroom. The walls are wainscotted, and a small door from the kitchen opens to the narrow stairway leading to the unfinished loft.

Upstairs, the stovepipe passes through the middle of the floor, and rope bunks line the southern wall. Part of the sloping ceiling is covered with newspapers from the thirties and some old cartoons from the Halifax *Chronicle-Herald* that I put up one summer. By the light of a small candle I'd settle into my bunk by the window as the spruce trees soughed in the wind. Early in the morning was the smell of the woodstove and the clumping of heavy boots on the kitchen floor as the birdwatchers set out for the day.

Slightly farther up the shore were two abandoned buildings and the remains of a wharf and slipway. We played in and around the old cookhouse and on the wharf, setting up forts and making plans to repair buildings already long past salvation. Today the buildings are gone and the wharf has been beaten apart by the sea. Beyond the old buildings, along the northwest shore were the landmarks we named: "Skidoo Rock," and the protruding "Farmer McGee's Bum" rock on the shingle beach below the Troll Camp. The camp was a rudely constructed affair of driftwood and old lobster traps, an outpost for imaginative Mills and McLaren children where mud pies, sun-bleached sheeps' skulls and long strands of kelp provided hours of entertainment. (The structure has since been rebuilt, and during my time as a lightkeeper on the island I made several journeys along the shore collecting driftwood to replace the rotting walls.)

The island was a paradise, with unlimited opportunities for exploration and discovery. We walked around the island, and up to Race Point on the northern end where the tide churned the green waters. Along the northeast shore we'd pass by the constantly eroding High Bank, looking down at the seals and bobbing eider ducks. Past the sheep-grazed bluff called Head Yard was the broad sand beach, backed by the marram-covered dunes.

Over the grassy hillocks, West Side Pond and the small cluster of houses above the cracked cement wharf shimmered in the heat of the afternoon. From the west side a rutted road ran to the east, its turf closely cropped by grazing sheep. The southern part of the island is covered in dense spruce woods and, to the north, sand dunes anchored with marram grass stretch to the other wooded half of the island. From some seaward points the island appears to be two small islands linked by a low grassy bar. On the west side, a shingle beach protects a large briny pond from the sea, and to the east the dunes guard the low marshy area in the middle.

At Little Head Yard on the southern end of the beach the rocky track led to the east and west sides. We'd walk by Brig Pond and below Ern and Judy's place up on the hill. Ernest Smith and his wife came to the island every year to spend most of the summer and fall in the old red house. We spent many evenings in the hot, brightly lighted kitchen, telling stories, playing cards and laughing until our insides hurt. Almost ten years later I visited regularly with the Smiths, bringing loads of firewood to the house with the lightstation tractor and cart, and enjoying fresh tea biscuits and coffee.

One evening I stopped in for a visit after a walk to the west side. Ern, a weathered old man with white forehead and hair standing up from wearing a ballcap all day, sat by the window in the gaslit kitchen. Beyond the window and through the

Near "High Bank," looking toward Race Point. *Chris Mills photo.*

Mrs. Hamilton's house. *Chris Mills photo.*

darkness the Cape light flashed, as he told me about the war and his time as a young soldier in Edinburgh and Glasgow. I got a peculiar feeling, sitting in the warm and bright room while Ern spoke of Vimy, Ypres and Leghorn. Fifty years had passed since that time, but all that Ern had seen was close that night.

Seal Island itself had not been far from wartime action. During the first war, the fishing boat owned by Winifred Hamilton's Uncle Sylvanus had been torpedoed by a German submarine as he fished near the island. Much to Winifred's surprise, her uncle and his oilskinned crew arrived at the lightstation one afternoon just after rowing from their unpleasant rendezvous with the enemy craft.

A quarter of a century later the 3,000-ton freighter *Liverpool Packet* was torpedoed by a German U-boat within fifteen miles of Seal Island. Two men were killed when the torpedo ripped through the *Packet*'s boiler room, but the rest of the crew escaped in a lifeboat. As the ship sank, the German submarine surfaced close to the lifeboat and, with guns trained on the survivors, the U-boat captain demanded to know the *Packet*'s destination and cargo. With this information received, it disappeared beneath the waves, leaving the overcrowded lifeboat alone on the sea. A day later a fishing boat picked up the men and took them to Seal Island where they received food and clothing before being taken to the mainland the next day.

In her book *B Was for Butter*, Evelyn Richardson noted one of the popular stories later told about the incident. As the crewmembers of the *Packet* launched the lifeboat or jumped into the water to escape the vortex created by the sinking ship, Captain Smith yelled to one of the young men, " 'Save the flag, Vernon, save the flag!' Vernon figured this was no time for heroics and symbols. 'Save it yourself, Cap'n!' he yelled back. Cap'n Norm did."

On the east side, beyond Ern and Judy's place on the hill, were a handful of old houses and fish stores. Several have disappeared now and two new houses have been built by Mary Nickerson and friend Eunice Smith. Set back from the shore and amongst the trees is the home to which Winifred Hamilton moved when she left the lighthouse, and where daugher Mary now lives with her husband and six dogs. I remember visiting Mrs. Hamilton in her house full of treasures from the island's past. She had glass cases full of photos, oil lamps, bottles, stuffed birds, and old pictures of the lighthouse from her childhood days. Although she left on a number of occasions to attend school in Yarmouth and to begin nurses' training, she spent the greater part of her life as the daughter and wife of lighthouse keepers and then as the guardian of the island she loved. In a 1932 article, Thomas Raddall called Winifred "the Dame of Seal Island," a fitting title for a woman who devoted nine decades to the care of her island home.

As a child she had witnessed hurricanes, walls of ice surrounding the island and many shipwrecks, often two or three in a year. She remembered picking up citrus fruit from the *Bambora*, wrecked on the Salvages near Port LaTour in 1894. The ship's cargo of thousands of boxes of lemons and oranges washed up along the miles of coastline, and children collected and carried home as much of the fruit as they could hold. The oranges were also popular with the sheep, who much preferred them over the sour lemons. " 'They'd get a lemon in their mouth and come down hard, then what a face! You should'a seen them screwin' their jaws around t'git rid of that lemon.' "[17]

Other wrecks were less bountiful. One night in the early months of 1900, Winnie's father had watched a coal-laden schooner to the north of the island as he prepared to light the lighthouse lamp for the evening. When he finished his work and looked to the north again, the ship had disappeared; there were no survivors. In 1918 the *Lewis Cottingham*, loaded with lumber, foundered southwest of the island. The keepers saw the ship from the lighthouse, and later a tug towed the lifeless vessel to the east side of the island, where it was beached; there

Leslie, Bernice and Winifred, children of John and Caroline (Thomas) Crowell. Photo taken on Light Road, school in background. *William M. Brauren, courtesy Mary Nickerson 1896.*

VANISHING LIGHTS

had also been no survivors. Today the ribs of the wooden vessel are occasionally visible on the east beach, as the constantly moving sands build and recede.

The remains of many shipwreck victims who were buried on the island have been lost over the years as the crumbling shoreline has been beaten away by the sea and wind. On the south point, just above "The Bar," three concrete headstones stand vigil over the final resting place of three unidentified women who died when the brig *Triumph* was wrecked on Blonde Rock in 1861. Thirty years later the Blonde claimed the life of Annie Lindsay, a stewardess on the SS *Ottawa*, caught on the rock in a southwest gale. Her body was brought to the island and buried. The simple wooden cross near the church which for many years marked her grave was later replaced with an inscribed concrete headstone, and it still stands today, overlooking the quiet east side.

In a small clearing above the cookhouse on the west side are two more graves: a cement headstone for Richard Charles Hichens Thomas, and a slab of granite marking the grave of a Mr. Hill, who had died on the island while looking for buried treasure. Richard Thomas had come to the island from England some years after the Hichens and Crowells had settled on the east and west sides. In 1881 his daughter Caroline married lightkeeper John Crowell. Her two brothers built homes at east side, one of which remains today. Known now as "the birdwatchers' house," it is owned by Mary Nickerson and used by visitors to the island during the summer months.

During Winifred Hamilton's life many changes occurred on Seal Island, not least of passing of the lighthouse from family care and the gradual dwindling of the resident population. During the first few decades of the twentieth century there had been the church, a general store, a lobster factory, a lifesaving station, a cable telephone link with the mainland, and a school on the island. By 1973 the post office was the only remaining service lingering from the days of permanent habitation. On September 29 of that year the Seal

Island post office was closed down by the Clark's Harbour postmaster, much to the chagrin of Winifred and the other island residents. "It is quite a blow to us all," she wrote, "you know what mail day means ... we have gone back to the dark ages."

Two years later, at the age of eighty-six, Winifred gained a modern amenity, though — for the first time in her life she received electric power in the small house. In 1974, American divers working around the island became aware of her desire for electricity, and the next year a path from the lighthouse to the east side was cleared and wires were laid. Winifred was then presented with several electric appliances, including a frying pan, hot plate, iron and kettle by the men who had worked to bring her home into the twentieth century. For the first time, the "flick of a switch" brought light and heat to the woman who had as a matter of course chopped wood and hauled water every day. Winifred Hamilton died on the island seven years later, in 1982.

Below Winifred's house and farther up the shore, lobster traps and empty bait barrels almost hide the east side boathouse and the slipway where the fishermen haul up their punts. Behind, the white steeple of the church stands against the gnarly spruce and blue sky. Caroline Crowell founded the church, raising the money for its construction with other island residents by organizing community suppers and quilting bees. The island was never home to a resident minister, but services were held by visiting mainland preachers who often made week-long visits to the island during the busy fishing season. Half a century has passed since regular Sunday school classes have been held there, but most summers bring at least one gathering of worshippers during Sunday outings from the mainland. As children we'd sign the guestbook at the small pulpit each time we visited the island, and today I look back on the names of scores of Cape Islanders interspersed with various Millses and McLarens.

Beyond the church, Saltwater Pond reeks of decaying

kelp and Irish moss between tides. A rough trail continues south along the shore and through the woods to Mother Owen's Point and its sand beaches. As a young boy, my route invariably took me not along the southern shore, but to the sheltered sandy track not far from the church — the road to the lighthouse. More a wide trail than a road, it meandered through moss-laden spruce trees to the southern end of the island. Countless tractor and cart journeys to and from the station had worn smooth ruts in the ground and a long strip of turf snaked in between. Much of the road had been built with several decades' worth of cinders from the old fog-whistle boilers and with sand and gravel laboriously hauled from the beaches.

Around each bend the sound of the station generators grew louder, and suddenly the main entrance to the lightstation was in view. One gate for the tractor and one for pedestrians — both red and white. Inside the gate and to the right stood a small white bungalow, once home to island radio operators.[18] With the departure of Steve Ahern, the last radio operator, the house was vacant for several years until lightkeeper Morris Swim and his wife Beulah took up residence. Although the house had been vacant for more than a decade when I arrived on the station in 1989, it was still known as "Morris's House."

Past the bungalow, the rutted lane continued to a small wooden bridge over swampy ground and to the lighthouse yard. To the left the domestic generator room with its roaring three-cylinder diesels and a large barn built by keeper Ellsworth Hamilton formed the east side of the lighthouse compound. In past years the barn had been used for hay and the cows, horses, pigs and hens kept by the Hamiltons. With the stalls knocked out, it served as a workshop and garage for the tractor. Ellsworth had built the barn himself at the not inconsiderable cost of $500; the government had "found the money" for the shingles.

The double keepers' dwelling, built in 1953 to replace the

original house, stood to the right of the barn with its green shutters and red roof. The lighthouse and paint shed were the only original structures remaining, completing the west side of the station.

I remember the old light, with its massive circular iron lantern and second-order classical lens. In 1902 it had replaced a fixed light lit by seal oil and, later, kerosene. The new light, lit by Abraham Gesner's kerosene in the vapour burner recently introduced by the Diamond Heating and Lighting Company of Montreal, sent three flashes sixteen miles out to sea every fifteen seconds. The vapour apparatus remained in use until 1959 when an electric light was installed in the large lens.

The change from kerosene to electricity brought to an end the time-consuming process of lugging fuel up the lighthouse steps in two-gallon cans and pumping up the pressure tanks, as well as an end to the constant watch of the keepers for "flaring." In her short account of the shipwrecks and lightkeepers of Seal Island, Winifred Hamilton noted that between 1902 and 1917 her father had not taken a single holiday from his work at the lighthouse, nor had he missed a single watch on the light or the steam fog whistle. The vapour light was difficult to operate and, as a result, John Crowell could find no one to relieve him of his duties at the lighthouse. Not long after the new light was installed in 1978, we journeyed out to the island and I can remember noting that the character and intensity of the flash had changed, even from our distant position several miles from the island.

In the field southwest of the lighthouse (known as the Mowing Field, where hay was grown for the livestock) was another relic from the past. Although the surrounding structure had long since been demolished, the old fog whistle boiler stood solid. Established in 1870 and replaced by a powerful diaphone in the first decade of the twentieth century, it continued to stand in the middle of its brick foundation. In the early 1980s, keeper Raymond Tiner painted most of the boiler black to slow the rusting process, and ten years later we

Sheep thrive on the island. Here, Max Hamilton poses with his pet lamb, Teddy. Old fog whistle building in background. *Mary Nickerson.*

were still using the firebox to burn our garbage.

Our electric horn, down by the shore on its aluminum tower, had superseded the steam whistle's own replacement not long before the second engine room had been torn down. In 1900, at the age of eleven, Winifred had watched the building being constructed, and seventy-five years later she watched as a Coast Guard crew tore it down. Although the massive wooden structure had been in excellent shape, it was declared surplus, its functions taken over by two cinder-block structures housing automated equipment. Gary Tiner, a Coast Guard diesel mechanic and son of lightkeeper Ray Tiner, commented that there had been a special atmosphere in the old whistle house,[19] with its polished floors and varnished wainscotting. The office with hardwood floors and radio equipment had been like a museum, he remembered, and there was always a big jar of bull's-eye candies on the desk. There was no such charm in the new flourescent-lit and steel-doored "cubes" built to replace the old building. Nonetheless, parts of the old structure live on. Mary Nickerson hauled some of the wood and windows from the old building to the east side and built a house with the seventy-five-year-old lumber.

It was with my childhood memories of island and lighthouse that I arrived on Seal Island as assistant lightkeeper in November 1989. I spent six twenty-eight-day shifts on the lightstation over a period of a year. A month before my first shift, I had visited the island for the first time in three years. During my stay a friend told me of an opening for an assistant keeper at the light and, although candidates were only required for two shifts, it was possible that there might be more work at the station in the new year. Not long after a successful interview with the Coast Guard at the employment centre in Shelburne, I stepped out of the helicopter with hope for the coming year.

Signs of the impending destaffing of the station were very much in evidence. A work crew had been at the lighthouse for several weeks, building a new engine room next to the tower. The engine and radio rooms on the shore, which had been built during the original automation program twenty years previously, would be demolished. The station yard was filled with bags of cement, sand and gravel, and cement mixers; and a backhoe had already dug up most of what had previously been lush green lawn. Our twice daily trips to the radio room at lighthouse roll-call time were made treacherous by a two-foot-deep trench running from the lighthouse to the shore.

By the late spring, the new engine room had been completed and the generators were on line. The control and power cables for the foghorn and radio beacon had finally been laid in the trench, and we had filled most of it in, planting grass seed on the long scar of dark earth. It was not until the summer that the station was once again presentable, with mowed lawns and a recently-built, white vinyl-sided engine room with its red door, air vents and exhaust pipes. The Coast Guard ship *Thomas Carleton* arrived at the island in the late spring with a load of two-by-four lumber for the fence around the station. Although the fence project had been started more than a year earlier, it had not been completed; and despite the threat of destaffing, we decided to finish the job. Throughout the winter and spring several of the island's 350 sheep, while nicely cropping the grass, had made the lawn a minefield of manure and we were keen to finish the fence and leave the sheep to fertilize the grass outside the station grounds.

By May, the Intrac system had been installed and tested. We were to be the last lightstation in the Bay of Fundy to be put on the lighthouse monitoring system based at Cape Forchu in Yarmouth. Now it was just a matter of time until we would be removed from the island. Nevertheless, we filled our days working around the station and visiting with islanders and tourists. We saw a fair number of people from Quebec, the UK, the USA and Europe. Many had never even seen a lighthouse before, let alone climbed to the top of one, and many questions were put to us about the workings of the light and horn. One woman asked me who was responsible for the operation of lighthouses in Canada, and when I said that they were public property, meaning government-run, she immediately walked over to our house and stepped inside. When I explained that we lived in the dwelling, and as such it was "private," she apologized, saying she thought the place was a museum. "Not far from the truth," I said. "We're the relics of a bygone age."

There were also visits from the locals — fishermen and mossers — many of whom had come to spend a week or two to rake moss or just relax. A strong tie exists between Cape Sable Islanders and Seal Island, spanning many generations. Administratively, Seal Island belongs to Yarmouth County, as do the Tusket Islands closer to the mainland, but historically the island's strongest ties have been with Cape Sable Island and Shelburne County. For more than two centuries, Cape Islanders have travelled to Seal to fish for pollock, cod, haddock and lobster, and more recently to harvest Irish Moss. In the mid-nineteenth century, James Symonds settled on the island. It is believed that James, like Richard Hichens, was shipwrecked on the ledges off Cape Sable and, again like Richard, decided to remain in the area. James lived at the lightstation for a number of years while Corning Crowell, Sr. was lightkeeper. By the first decade of the twentieth century, James' son Thomas was fishing for lobster from the east side and held the position of coxswain of the island lifeboat. Today grandson Doug and wife Geraldine have a small house at the west side where they spend a good part of the summer and fall. Doug lobstered from the island until 1991, and his sons continue to fish from the island during the lobster season.

Another Symonds, Charles, was born on the island in 1924 and spent almost four decades of his life there. Upon leaving Seal Island he settled on nearby Cape Sable as assistant lightkeeper. In 1979, one year after his retirement, his son-in-law Brian became assistant keeper on the Cape. From Cape Sable, Brian and Sherrill moved to Bon Portage, the island made famous by Evelyn Richardson's *We Keep A Light*. When the light was fully automated in 1984, the Stoddard family moved to the island where Sherrill's father had been born sixty years before. By the summer of 1986, though, the lightkeepers' families had been removed from Seal Island, and the station changed to rotational bachelor status. I worked with Brian Stoddard for the better part of a year at the lighthouse and learned of his family's love of the island lights they had helped keep. Not long before the lighthouse was automated, Sherrill and the children journeyed to the island for a last visit to what had been their home for two years. At the end of the day it was hard to leave, knowing that the place would soon be abandoned.

Many other Cape Islanders have close ties with Seal

Island and, although the settlements on the east and west sides no longer boast year-round populations, the grandchildren and great grandchildren of fishermen and lightkeepers continue to travel to the island every year. Mossers and birdwatchers frequent the island in the summer and early fall, living on the west and east sides. A handful of dwellings and fish sheds are used during the lobster season by fishermen from Cape Sable Island; they use a large cookhouse on the island to save travelling the eighteen miles back and forth to the mainland every day.

On summer evenings the west side cove is filled with moored fishing boats and, if the tide if right, the small punts of the Irish mossers can be seen dotted around the shore. The seaweed (*Chondrus crispus*) is harvested with the use of long rakes from the boats and then dried and bagged. Carrageenin is the principal commercial product rendered from the bushy seaweed; it is used in pharmaceuticals and as a thickener in dairy products and soups. The reddish moss grows in the middle intertidal zone between rockweeds and kelp, and raking it is hard work, especially with the constant bending and hauling required to pull the moss from the rocks. Although some moss is sold wet, most is dried and bagged with the expectation of higher market prices in the fall. Spread out to dry amongst the scattered boulders on the short-cropped grass of the east and west sides, it fills the air with a pungent, salty aroma.

Sheep wander amongst the buildings and rock-studded ground. Although the island was named for the great number of seals observed around its shores (during the seventeenth century seal hunters came to the island from the French settlement of Port Royal), in recent years the sheep has been the prodominant mammal. Seals are still common around the island and are much disliked by fishermen whose nets and catch suffer the hungry mammal's powerful jaws and sharp teeth.

Local folklore states that sheep have been on Seal Island

and several other islands off the southwest coast of Nova Scotia for two centuries or more and that they were originally placed there for the benefit of hungry shipwrecked mariners. Today most of the 250 sheep on Seal are kept for their wool, and a few for market. In the summer they are herded with sheepdogs and sheared in pens set up on the east side. Rams are taken off in the late summer and returned to the island in December so breeding will produce lambs in the spring and not during the cruel winter.

The sheep are a particularly hardy breed, essentially wild and able to withstand the harsh island environment. On my frequent walks around the island, I encountered sheep on the beaches with long ribbons of brown kelp hanging from moving jaws as they stared at me with baleful eyes. Kelp forms a large part of the island sheep diet — from late autumn to early summer they feed almost exclusively on the subtidal foliage tossed ashore by winter's storms.

I spent many hours walking around the island, exploring the woods and visiting my favourite haunts. Although I enjoyed the work we did on the station, I found it necessary to get away from the activity and noise of the lighthouse compound. Halfway through a particularly foggy shift I noted in my journal the symphony of sound on the station:

This place is noisy. Sitting in the kitchen now I hear a variety of sounds — the TV in the living room, the perpetual kettle on low burner on the stove, kitchen clock ticking away and the omnipresent rumble of the domestic generator. Down at the shore the lighthouse generator's percussive exhaust beats in a non-ending tattoo, while in the tower the main light grinds in slow circles. Once in a while the furnace comes on, muting the staccato of the VHF radio next to the sink. And then the fog rolls in and everything is conducted by the regular blasts of the horn.

Behind the lighthouse, under dripping spruce trees, I walked along Cameron's Road toward the east side. Lighthouse builder Mr. Cameron, with the help of a sturdy horse, had hauled much of the lumber used in the construction of the tower along this trail from the east side, where it had been landed after being floated from the mainland. Off Cameron's Road are narrow trails leading to the southwest shore's swampy shoreline and to the west side settlement.

The woods are thick and dark, with little sunlight permeating the tangled branches hung with Old Man's Beard. On the east side behind the hill overlooking Brig Pond is a small valley filled with large boulders; in past years, trees formed a canopy overhead. Wizard's Glen was a dark and mysterious place, with small caves amongst the rocks and dark holes in the peaty forest floor. Some of the trees are gone now, but a century or more ago it was a shady, secret spot. It was here that the Thomas family had hidden from a band of marauding Fenians according to an account passed down through generations of the Crowell-Hamilton family.[20]

The story goes that Caroline Crowell ran to the east side and the lighthouse to warn the Thomases and the keepers that Fenian "raiders" had landed on the west side. With the Crowells behind locked doors at the lighthouse, and the Thomas family hidden in Wizard's Glen, Mr. Hichens reportedly held off the Fenians with a pitchfork in his barn on the west side. Apparently he was successful in defending the island, although the raiders were able to secure Hichens' dog and a barrel of corned beef before they departed the island![21]

Secret clearings may be found throughout the island's interior. Woods paths cut across the island from many openings in the dense trees. And there are many false entrances, made by sheep seeking shelter from winter winds. Along the northern and southern shores the trees appear to have been limbed to three or four feet, creating labyrinths, apparently designed for a race of short and privacy-seeking woods dwellers. Along the northwest shore the trees are so thick that you can walk on top of them. Not far from the North

Home, the remains of a fishing boat that broke its moorings and smashed on the shore with its skipper still aboard can still be seen scattered along the beach and up along the edge of the thick spruce.

Other walks took me through the centre of the island, along narrow paths where the sunlight could not penetrate the moss-hung spruce trees. Sometimes I felt as though I was being watched, but when I looked around there was never anyone or anything to be seen. The island has a large population of cats, originally brought over by fishermen and left to go wild. Nine kittens were born on the lightstation during the summer of 1990, adding to the largely unseen population in the surrounding woods.

The only time we saw the wild cats was in the winter when they came around the lightstation looking for food. Near dusk one day I saw one that looked like a miniature panther, jet black against the new fallen snow. Others slunk around the old whistle boiler, nosing through our burned garbage. When our mama cat was in heat she attracted a fair number of tomcats to the lighthouse, intent on romance. The station tom (imaginatively named Tom) guarded his territory jealously, "putting the run" to any intruding rivals. During my nightly rounds one spring evening, I happened upon Tom and a battle-scarred competitor in the domestic engine room, engaged in what appeared to be a fight to the death. I could hear their screeches over the roar of the generator as they thrashed about on the floor. Finally the would-be usurper decided that he had had enough and made for the open door and the woods beyond.

My favourite haunt was the south point of the island known as The Bar (Mother Owens Point). Through the narrow woods path I'd walk to the three graves overlooking the wall of beach stone meeting at point. On either side of the point, the sand beach was constantly changing: one day a broad expanse of sand, the next a shingle beach covered with large smooth granite stones. On nights bright with a full moon, I'd walk from the station down to the fog alarm and along the beach:

> The track to the SE point above the sand beach is rocky and rutted. I pass the raucous beat of the lighthouse engine and the flashing eye of the fog detector. As the sound of the generators recedes and mingles with that of the surf, the light shows its broad sweep over the breakers at the point. An almost full moon shimmers on the sea, and the shores are lightly wreathed in sea smoke. Off the point the waves meet, explode and fall back into themselves. The sun has now gone, leaving only a faint orange glow beyond the darkening seas.

By September it was time for me to leave the island. For four months the Intrac had been working more or less as it should, sending electronic reports to the long-distance keepers at Cape Forchu while we readied ourselves for the final departure. Brian would be assigned as a crewman on the Clark's Harbour Coast Guard cutter, a job that would not take him from his family for month-long periods and would enable him to be close to home most of the time. Shortly before my departure on September 12, I learned that I would have two weeks ashore and then travel to another Seal island, New Brunswick's Machias Seal, for a month-long shift. Mary and Jim Nickerson would not be spending the winter in their east side home; with the lightkeepers gone, emergency assistance during the depths of winter would be less assured.

Nonetheless, Mary Hichens' lighthouse continues to flash into storm-darkened days and is a tribute to the families who came to save the lives of seafarers and to make the island home.

Puffins, Machias Seal Island. *Photo by Bob Boudreau.*

99

FIVE
Machias Seal Island:
Christmas & Controversy

It's a beautiful little island, all grass and birds like you
wouldn't believe — Basil Small[22]

Why Fight Over Bleak Little Island?
Saint John *Telegraph Journal*, May 7, 1988

AS WE approached the small, crescent-shaped island halfway
between Maine and New Brunswick, I heard Reg Smith's voice
in the chopper headphones. "Be it ever so humble ... " he said,
leaving the phrase unfinished. Although he's on the island only
five months out of twelve, he considers the place home. Since
1986 when the station changed from family to bachelor status,
four lightkeepers have kept the light, two at a time on twenty-
eight-day shifts. Reg came to the island six years ago,
continuing a lightkeeping career that began in 1944 when he
moved to the Cape Sable light with his family. His father was a
thirty-two-year veteran of the lights upon his retirement, and
Reg himself has spent fourteen years as a full-time keeper, not
including part-time work on the lights between 1944 and 1978.

Prior to his posting on Machias Seal he had worked on six
lighthouse islands along the southwest coast of Nova Scotia;
his attachment to lightkeeping was obvious and he seemed to

me well cut out for the job, being of suitable outlook and temperament. This was my third island in almost two years and my second shift on Machias Seal. Although I faced the prospect of spending Christmas, my birthday and New Year's on the treeless six-hectare island, I was happy to be returning after spending an extra twenty-eight days ashore because of a shortage of lightkeeping positions.

Having worked on the island in the autumn and winter, my experience of Machias Seal Island has been different than most people's. Between May and late August, island life is ruled by the presence of the seabirds that breed there: some 5,000 Atlantic Puffins, Leach's Storm-Petrels, Razorbills, and Arctic and Common Terns. (Since 1944, Machias Seal Island has been a migratory bird sanctuary under the control of the Canadian Wildlife Service.) At the end of spring, with winter's gales a fading memory, the tiny island comes alive with wheeling, screeching birds and the tourists and naturalists who come to see them. The lightkeepers tailor their daily work to the arrival of the tour boats from Grand Manan and Maine, mowing the lawns and painting during the late afternoons and evenings when the tourists have left.

But the biggest change in the keepers' routine comes when the Canadian Wildlife Service warden arrives in late May. From that time until the end of the breeding season, the keepers and the visitors are confined to the mowed areas around the lightstation and to the paths leading to the blinds along the shore so disturbance of the nesting sites is kept to a minimum. The shoreline becomes off limits, and the walks around the island favoured by keepers are postponed until the end of summer.

Over the years, the impact of human residents and visitors to the island has been increasingly questioned and studied; concerns have been raised that human disturbances of the nests have resulted in a higher than usual mortality rate for tern chicks.[23] By the mid-1980s the number of visitors during breeding season was limited to thirty per day, causing a

The light's glowing tower at dusk. *Chris Mills photo.*

not inconsiderable amount of friction between the two principal tour-boat operators. Much to the annoyance and disappointment of his paying customers, Preston Wilcox often had to return to Grand Manan from the island without having been able to let anyone ashore, because the quota of visitors had already been filled by the Maine tour-boat operator. Eventually though, a compromise was reached, allowing each boat approximately half the visitor quota.

Although the activities of the seabirds have set Machias Seal apart from other Bay of Fundy lighthouse establishments, the political controversy surrounding the island makes it a place of singular character. Much of the island's notoriety has resulted not from the environmental sensitivity of the breeding grounds, but from contested ownership of the land itself. The controversy around the sovereignty issue, although long-standing, has become prominent only in the last few decades. In the 1970s disputes between New Brunswick and Maine fishermen in the surrounding waters began to arouse political and media interest. One particular incident in 1972 involving a Maine fisherman and a Canadian Fisheries Patrol boat was highly publicized. As the fisherman hauled lobster traps near the island, the patrol boat came alongside and informed him that he was in Canadian waters and should leave the area at once. Upon his return to home port, the fishermen contacted his congressman, and so the dispute, which had for so long been forgotten, surfaced once again.

Throughout the 1970s and 1980s the island's rediscovered "political sensitivity" provided fodder for American and Canadian politicians and interested individuals who saw an opportunity to jump on the sovereignty bandwagon. The Canadian claim to Machias Seal Island, based mainly on the presence of a lighthouse and lightkeepers since 1832 was seen as invalid by the proponents of U.S. ownership,[24] while an interpretation of the 1783 Treaty of Paris provided the basis for belief in American claims to the land. Although several Bay of Fundy islands including Grand Manan, Deer and Campobello were given to Great Britain with the signing of the Treaty of Ghent in 1814, other smaller islands to the south remained within U.S. territory, including, "by intent, if not by name," Machias Seal Island.

In recent years, Barna Norton, a tour-boat operator from Jonesport, Maine, has claimed that the island has been owned by his family for more than one hundred years, having been deeded to his great grandfather, Barney Beal, in 1865.

According to Maine lore, "Tall Barney" was a giant man, who had little patience for argument:

> He knew no fear and slight restraint,
> When others frothed or made complaint,
> But settled every quarrel quick,
> With energetic kick or lick.

Parallels with today's political situation are evident throughout a long poem composed in his honour. When Britain accused Barney of fishing too close to colonial holdings and attempted to arrest him,

> Five men then tried the bold affront
> To Barney's frame. He faced the brunt
> Of battle, broke one sword,
> Tossed the leader overboard,

> And sent the other hostile four
> Asprawl upon the vessel's floor,
> With clothes ripped off to gory skin
> And muskets smashed, to their chagrin.[25]

Recent disagreements between the United States and Canada have been less bloody but based on the same conflict. Several incidents in the mid-1980s involving the Canadian Wildlife Service, the RCMP, the U.S. State Department and American senators heightened the tension between American and Canadian proponents. In addition, concerns were voiced increasingly throughout the eighties about the effects of Canadian Coast Guard activities on and around the island, particularly the helicopter that was said to have killed several birds when they flew into its rotors. In 1986, Norton formed the "U.S. Territory of Machias Seal Islands" to further back the claim of U.S. ownership and held several annual meetings on the island, raising and pledging allegiance to the Stars and Stripes. Norton goes as far as to state in his tour-boat pamphlets that "The Canadian claim to the island because of

00344

My name is Laura Amanda Norton, I am 91 years old

My grandfather was Barna Beal (Tall Barney) In the Spring of 1865 he stopped the take over by Canadian Officers of the Territory of Machias Seal Island and its surrounding fishing grounds. When boarded by these men who were going to arrest Barna and crew, he threw them overboard and drove them back to Grand Manan. Once again upholding ownership of Machias Seal Island which he claimed. He was very anxious that the fog signal and light remain there and frequently carried supplies to the Keepers.

As a small girl a promise was made to me by my grandfather that the first child that I had should be named for him. If so, the ownership of Machias Seal Island would pass to the child. On June 9th, 1915, my son Barna Beal Norton was born – named Barna Beal Norton — very soon after the event John A. Beal, oldest son of Till Barna, came to me and brought up the subject of the agreement and as administrator of his father's estate declared that the ownership of Machias Seal Island belonged to my son: Barna Beal Norton. He in turn has defended his right to ownership for over 40 years.

L. Amanda Norton,

Barna Beal Norton
L. Amanda Norton.

State of Maine

County of Washington

Date January 1, 1965

Personally appeared the above named L. Amanda Norton who acknowledged the foregoing instrument by her subscribed to be her free act and deed

Notary Public

DAVID E. ALLEY
NOTARY PUBLIC
My Commission Expires June 30, 1966

Enclosed in a letter to the author was this statement by Laura Amanda Norton of her belief in her son's claim to ownership of Machias Seal Island.

her lighthouse has No merit. (International Court Minquiers and Ecrehos Case — 1953)."

In 1987 the Canadian Wildlife Service stated that its permits would be required to land on the island, regardless of whether visitors were from the United States or Canada. This did not sit well with Norton, who had been told by the U.S. State Department in 1983 that "You have every right to ignore any regulations that Canada might pretend to set for Machias Seal Island." The consequent media attention brought the tiny island into the international spotlight and more people in both Canada and the USA became concerned about the ownership of an island that had until that point been unknown except to lightkeepers and some Mainers and Grand Mananers.

Nevertheless, despite unequivocal beliefs on either side of the border that the island is theirs, the dispute has not yet been formally resolved. Tour boats from Maine and New Brunswick continue to bring crowds of curious visitors to see the colourful puffins and terns, while the lightkeepers serve their four week vigils. One result of the dispute over the island's sovereignty is that the lightstation will remain staffed indefinitely — a rare reprieve for a Canadian, or any, lighthouse in the closing years of the twentieth century.

Oblivious to the sporadic wrangling of politicians and the media, the birds continue to breed, feed and, at the end of the summer, migrate. During the summer the island is inundated with a cacophony of sight and sound and smell. The terns not only nest in the long grass that covers most of the island, but on the station lawn, under the boardwalks and around the helicopter pad. Along the shoreline the granite is permanently stained with puffin guano. The air is filled with the heady reek of the stuff, and with the shrill cries of thousands of wheeling birds. The noise is so great that while I was working on Gannet Rock I could hear the screeching through my VHF receiver as I spoke with the Machias keepers.

Over the years the lightkeepers on Machias Seal Island have taken a keen interest in the activities of the birds. In the

In winter the island has an empty, desolate beauty (above). *Chris Mills photo.* In summer it becomes a thriving bird colony (below). *Bob Boudreau photo.*

1960s and 1970s, before the imposition of formal regulations, Jack Russell began restricting island visitors from certain areas during the breeding season. Despite the presence of the Canadian Wildlife Service warden in the summer months, present-day keepers continue to keep an eye on both the bird and visitor populations. Most have enjoyed observing the birds in their natural habitat. In his six years on the station, Reg Smith has watched and noted the antics of the Arctic Terns and Atlantic Puffins as they have bred and raised their young on and around the island.

Atlantic Puffins have traditionally been described as having tragicomic faces and actions, and incidents on Machias backed this popular description. In 1989 several redundant buildings on the lightstation were burned down, including two large structures on the southern end of the island. One of these structures, the old fog alarm, had for many years been a favourite haunt of the puffins. Each morning they would gather on the ridge of the roof, sometimes 150 at a time. Apparently the birds thought that there was always room for one more, and when a newcomer would land in the middle of the line, one or two unfortunate birds would be bumped off the end of the roof, to the ground. On another occasion Reg was startled when a curious puffin, who had with its comrades been observing Reg work, fell off the edge of the roof of the oil shed, landing next to him. "I think it scared me more than it did the bird!" he said.

When Reg and partner Allan Stuart first began work on the island in 1986, they agreed on a routine that sent Allan down to the old engine room every evening to pump up the daytank for the generator while Reg gave the evening weather report. One evening, Allan got ready to "pump up," and as he left the house, Reg mentioned that maybe he should wear a hard hat because he would have to pass close to four or five tern nests around the helicopter pad. Terns are notoriously protective of their nesting grounds and will strike at intruders. Allan decided not to wear the suggested hat, opting instead to

Snow covered walkway linking the station and the slipway.
Chris Mills photo.

wave his arm over his head if threatened by any airborne bombers.

As he made down the boardwalk to the southern end of the island, a tern began diving at him. Well, it wasn't long before Allan received a well-aimed splatter of droppings on his hand. As he shook away the mess, the tern made another pass, this time striking Allan on the top of his head with its beak. Back at the house, Reg watched the attack with great amusement until he learned that the bird had actually drawn blood from his partner. After the incident, both keepers began wearing hard hats with attached flags to ward off the aggressive birds.

By the first of August, the nesting activity has pretty well ended and the restrictions on the number of daily visitors are lifted. Power cruisers and sailboats anchor on the east side and the crews come ashore, sometimes sixty people in a day. Autumn brings relief to the keepers, because they are once again left to the solitude of island life and to an uninterrupted routine of mowing and painting. During my first shift on the island we mowed the lawn through October, and the next shift of keepers cut it well into November. It seemed to grow exceptionally fast; hardly had we put the mowers away and the green was ankle deep and ready to be tackled again.

By late November, though, the grass is dead; autumn gales have lashed the greenery with salt and everything turns brown. I spent many of my evenings in the vacant keepers' house (used in the summers by the Canadian Wildlife Service warden) writing in my journal and listening to the radio. My notes describe one calm evening:

The full moon glitters on the water, as Southwest Head and Gannet Rock blink in the distance. A very peaceful evening, seemingly far removed from the noise and pressure of mainland life. Out of the corner of my eye I see our light flashing in the entry way windows and outside the smell of the last cutting of the lawn and the dry spice of autumnal weeds mingles with the salt of the surrounding air. I'm sitting in one of a tiny cluster of lighted buildings around a white tower on what is essentially a rock, halfway between Maine and New Brunswick. An endless stream of Principal and assistant keepers, along with their families have worked and lived in this environment of contrasts for 160 years. Autumn breezes, incessant fogs and winter's howling gales have accompanied the families as they tended the light, kept gardens and fished around the island.

Now the families are gone — in their place bachelor crews arrive every four weeks (weather permitting) by helicopter with supplies of canned goods, frozen meat, sacks of potatoes and boxes of bread and eggs. The gardens have grown over, and no one fishes anymore — there hasn't been a boat on the station for more than a decade. The television provides welcome relief from the tedium of long winter days, as does the hobby of wood-burning or painting. The long winter shifts are not necessarily conducive to healthy habits, as countless cigarettes, cups of coffee and snacks in front of the TV are respectively smoked, drunk and consumed. On more than one occasion a keeper's supply of cigarettes has run out before the end of a shift, resulting in a frantic search for all available tobacco on the island, including the contents of numerous ashtrays. One keeper, after smoking all of the tobacco in last week's butts, moved on to lawn clippings and tea, but found them somewhat inferior in quality to blended Virginia.

The change from year-round to rotational staffing has made lightkeeping on Machias Seal and other islands more of a job than a way of life. In the past, families maintained their lightstations as homes, lavishing time and effort on the upkeep of gardens, fences and paths as well as the lighthouse buildings. In recent years the twenty-eight-day shift has become a period of time in which you eat, sleep, do your work and then get ready to go home. Working on an island or a rock for five or six months out of every twelve also has an interesting way of cutting time into neat little chunks, which seems to make a year pass so much more quickly than usual. There are good shifts and bad shifts. Generally the best ones are in the late summer and early fall when clear dawns and mild temperatures allow the keepers to spend as much time as possible outdoors. The winter shifts are long, especially when howling winds and sub-zero temperatures make work outside difficult and uncomfortable.

Christmas on the island: J.R. Smith carves the turkey. *Chris Mills photo.*

Perhaps the worst shift is the one which comes during the Christmas season. It is difficult to be away from family and friends at the time of year when everyone seems to be getting together. Nonetheless, I found it pleasant to be far removed from the commercialism and bustle that now characterize the season. As we prepared to celebrate Christmas on the island, I thought about a phone call I received from a friend on the mainland during my first shift on Machias Seal. During our conversation she suggested that I was becoming a recluse by remaining on the lights. I had to agree, but not wholeheartedly. There is something about lightkeeping that gets into your blood, and even at the most social time of year I was glad to be experiencing island rather than mainland life.

Our preparations for Christmas were simple. We installed the Christmas tree: a delux two-foot plastic model, complete with lights and bobbles, and I put a string of lights around my bedroom window. Christmas Eve day dawned windy and wet with southwesterly gusts of thirty-five to forty knots. In the fog and rain the island was ringed by breakers, and from my room I could see the mare's tales off the northern end, and the explosions as the east and west waves met off the point. I tuned in the BBC World Service on my short-wave radio and listened to the lessons and carols from King's College Chapel in Cambridge as the blasts of the foghorn rattled the windows and the rain poured down.

Towards the evening, the wind veered to the northwest, increasing to forty-five knots and we heard from one of the keepers on Gannet Rock that a boat had been lost in the Yarmouth area. The search and rescue helicopter had found some wreckage and picked up one body. A tragedy at any time of year, but especially bad at Christmas. Later in the evening my sister called from Queensland, Australia, where she was working on a farm. It was amusing to hear of her efforts to describe to the operator where her call was being placed — a tiny island some 14,000 kilometres from Queensland, halfway around the world! It was Christmas morning for her, with overcast skies and a temperature of thirty-five degrees, a far cry from our northwest gale and two-degree chill! Our Christmas Day was clear and cold. Reg cooked a huge turkey with all the trimmings. The smell of dressing and the sound of Frank Sinatra on the radio singing "Silent Night" mingled to create a strong feeling of Christmases past. We ate turkey and stuffing and vegetables until we could eat no more, finishing the dinner with canned carrot cake and canned thick cream, washed down with mugs of hot tea. Reg's wife sent greetings to him on CJLS radio in Yarmouth, and we heard that two bodies of the missing fishermen from Sandford had now been found along with wreckage; a third man was still missing. He was never found.

The remainder of the shift was uneventful. We had several days of extremely cold weather, with wind chill factors of minus thirty to minus forty degrees. We spent our workdays painting in the Canadian Wildlife Service house, pumping oil for the furnace — a tedious process made uncomfortable by the icy winds — and writing up the year-end reports on oil consumption and foghorn and generator running times. In the evenings we watched TV and invariably played three or four games of pool after the seven-thirty radio schedule. A keeper had brought the pool table to the island, slung under a chopper, a decade earlier and since that time it had provided countless hours of enjoyment. The chipped balls and warped cues did not matter to us, because we improvised and altered the rules each evening.

But some evenings the pool table and TV were not enough to satisfy the desire to pass time in a constructive manner, and once in a while I would wander around aimlessly, wondering what I could do to occupy my time. Lighthouse life in the 1990s is very much what an individual makes it, since there is so little to do that is essential for the operation of the station. In some ways the best days are those which start and end the shift. As you approach the station, the whole island is laid out below you, neat buildings and flashing eye in the tower. This is when you are a lightkeeper: stepping from the chopper, transferring and stowing your food and gear and taking the first look around the station.

For the next twenty days or so you enter into the steady routine, where all tasks, small and large, are important. The final week is slow, eager with expectation of shift-change day. With keepers' gear aboard, the chopper leaves behind the outpost on the island and the men step ashore on airport tarmac. Once ashore, with kit unloaded, life resumes mainland pace, as the events of the past twenty-eight days are digested and put into perspective.

I often found it difficult to distance myself from my work and surroundings while on Machias, not only because of the island's small size, but because of the difficulty in remaining objective about the whole situation. Prior to becoming a

One of many chores: cleaning the main light. *Chris Mills photo.*

lightkeeper, I had thought that the sight of the white and red tower and buildings against the sea would always inspire in me the same feelings of awe and excitement, but after two years on the lights I was beginning to take my surroundings for granted. It was only during my time ashore that I could once again feel the same lure and excitement of the lights and islands. Nonetheless, my feelings of familiarity with lightkeeping only deepened my attachment to island life. An entry from my journal reveals this:

> When the winds are calm and after the fridge cuts out, the house is silent, almost dormant until two or three in the morning when the other keeper awakens for the early watch. The steady grumble of the big diesel in the lighthouse changes frequency as electric heaters cut in and out. The radio room is silent except for the electric hum of the wind gauge on the wall and the steady tick of the alarm clock on the desk. Outside the southeast breeze freshens, and lightly buffets the house. Every three seconds the bright shaft of the main light races across the tall grasses and the shore; for an instant, darkness is held at bay. Through the kitchen I can see the regular flash of the lighthouse at Southwest Head on Grand Manan, and 14 miles east of us, Gannet Rock's gleam on the horizon.

> The speaker on the radio room wall buzzes, and a clear voice calls "Machias Seal Island, this is Gannet Rock, you around Chris?" It is one of the two keepers on the rock for this Christmas shift. We exchange news (usually there isn't much) and talk about everything under the sun — lightkeeping, what's on TV, places seen and visited and, of course, the weather. Weather is probably the only topic which can be discussed day in and day out without becoming stale. The weather is ever changing and is a prime target for speculation, especially when "the barograph's right off the scale" or "she's blowin' a good puff tonight." I once asked one of the keepers on Gannet

Rock how big the seas got in stormy weather, and he replied that he kept a set of scuba tanks in his bedroom, just in case!

As the night wears on, the wind picks up and the noisy fridge cuts in again. It's midnight and although my shift has ended at 2200 hours I'm not yet ready to turn in. The evening routine has been finished; flags lowered for the night, lights out in the vacant keepers' house next door, radio schedule with Yarmouth Coast Guard Radio, and the engines wiped clean of oil, daytank checked. Tomorrow's routine will not vary greatly, although for variety there will be some painting to do next door and time for a couple of walks around the shore. If the weather's decent and there's not too much of a sea the lobster boats from Jonesport and Cutler will be out hauling and baiting traps, while the lightkeepers go about their own business on the small island.

Despite the long periods of solitude on Machias Seal Island, there are times when the place is abuzz with activity. Besides the arrival of the birds and the tour boats in the early summer, there are regular visits by Coast Guard mechanics and technicians, who inspect and service the navigation equipment. Helicopter visits, though often unannounced, are welcome, as they bring contact with other people after two weeks or more when the only other person you've seen is your partner. Now that the boats are gone, the chopper is the sole link with the mainland. Its sound inspires a variety of emotions, depending on the time of day and whether or not you're at the end of your four weeks on the station. During a shift, it invariably arrives just as you're sitting down to lunch, and the arrival of other people does tend to disrupt any work the keepers may be doing. While the techs do inspections or repair work, you usually stick around in case they need assistance or information.

Nonetheless, the diversion of unexpected visits is a

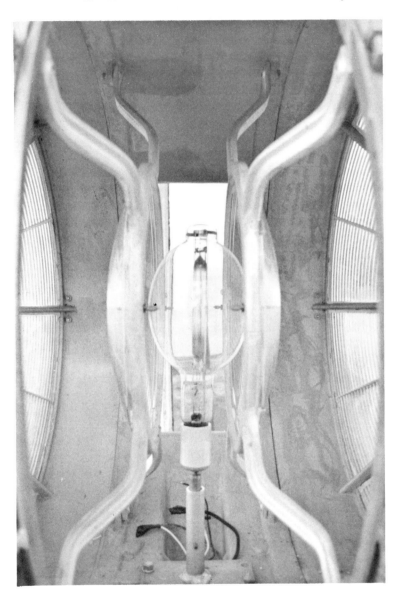

An inside view of the main light showing 1000 w Mercury Vapour bulb. *Chris Mills photo.*

welcome one. When the work is done, there is time for a coffee or tea in the house and chance to catch up on the latest Coast Guard news and gossip. During my two years as a lightkeeper in the Saint John district of the Coast Guard, I met most of the people who serviced the Bay of Fundy lights and horns — technicians, electricians, construction workers and mechanics. For the larger construction jobs, the work crews usually stay with the keepers on the station, adding some variety to the keeper's routine, sometimes for weeks at a time.

On Machias Seal, with a second house vacant most of the year, it was convenient for the workers to set up house and live in relative comfort during the job. To the east on Gannet Rock the situation was a little different, with only one eight-room house, and sometimes up to six workers staying on the station with the lightkeepers. Despite cramped conditions, even on Machias, it was enjoyable to sit around in the evening, playing cards, telling lies and slightly off-colour stories — true lighthouse culture indeed. And when the work was finished, it was also good to have life return to normal after days or weeks of constant demolition or construction.

The refuelling of lightstations is also a busy time, although not nearly as labour-intensive as in the past. Before the days of helicopters, fuel was brought ashore in barrels on small boats or barges and moved by hand to be pumped into the main storage tanks. Until recently, fuel oil transfers were accomplished by running hoses from a Coast Guard ship anchored off the island or a barge at the slipway to the lighthouse tanks. It was a dirty process which often allowed a great deal of water to get into the station fuel tanks. This method has now been superseded by the use of 150-gallon inflatable bladders which are flown between a nearby Coast Guard ship and the lightstation. Full bladders are pumped into the main tanks while empty ones are flown back to the ship to be filled.

Refuelling on Machias usually takes place twice a year, although the 12,000 gallons on the station can keep the twenty-five-kilowatt diesel generator running for more than a year. The amount of fuel consumed by the engines depends very much on the weather, since the operation of the electric heaters and the foghorn places an extra load on the system. The Christmas shift was a cold one, and we kept the baseboard heaters going full blast in an attempt to warm the drafty dwelling; a difficult task in a structure exposed to the wind from all directions. During periods of thick weather, the horn puts an additional load on the engines and, as it blasts, the frequency of the big engine changes.

Undoubtedly the foghorn is another important element of Machias Seal Island's character, one which sets it apart from other lightstations. In my opinion, the issues of sovereignty and the bird sanctuary paled in comparison to the issue of the horn. It was a singular horn, not in its signal or type, but in its position relative to the living quarters of the lightkeepers. One 1,000-watt emitter pointed west, and the other 1,000-watt emitter pointed east — directly at the house. (Later I would work on Gannet Rock, where the horn was mounted over our dwelling, but it came nowhere close to matching the horrendous blasts of the beast on Machias. One keeper was fond of calling it "that blattin' bastard," especially during the endless summer fogs.) My notes describe the conditions in the house during the operation of the horn:

> When the foghorn is on, the noise level around here is horrific. It's tolerable in my east-facing bedroom, but almost painful anywhere in the livingroom and western bedrooms. A couple of years ago someone from the Coast Guard brought a sound level meter to the island to measure the sound of the fog signal in the dwelling. In the livingroom an impressive level of 97 decibels was achieved! I find that if I sit in the easy chair by the front window my right ear begins to ring within an hour. The windows vibrate with each blast, adding to the nearly tenable sensation in my ears. The sound of a foghorn so

close day after day is aggravating, to say nothing of the annoyance it causes while we chat or watch TV. Two three second blasts every minute is extremely effective in obliterating all conversation, both on the TV and in the room.

But this was nothing compared to the shock of the first blast of the horn, especially at night when I couldn't see the fog rolling in. After a particularly foggy day ("thick as Aunt Maggie's quilt," Reg would say) the weather cleared, and during the evening I settled in on the couch to read a book and enjoy the silence. It was almost the end of my shift and all was quiet; radio silent, TV shut down for the night, fridge off. As I began to read, I noted with some satisfaction that the strong wind of the day had died and could hardly be heard. The distant tick of the alarm clock in the radio room was comforting, and the book engrossing. Alas, my peace and contentment were not to last. With a sudden, painful explosion, the horns started up, lifting me, it seemed, a full six inches from the couch. Heart pounding, ears ringing and muttering curses, I abandoned my book and retreated to my bedroom, where a thick pillow and silicone earplugs awaited me.

Although the noise of the horn was loud in the house, it was shattering in the yard. In front of the house the vibrations of 300 hertz made your chest vibrate and caused pain in the ears if you were not wearing ear protectors. The only way to escape the piercing blasts was to find somewhere upwind to wander. On average the station has 2,000 hours (80 days) of thick fog a year.

Generally the foggiest months are June and July, although August can be bad as well. Fog is not as common through the winter as it is in the spring and summer, but the horn is often on, blasting into the cold wisps of "sea smoke" which form when the relatively warm water meets the frigid air. The wind chill when the air temperature is minus sixteen degrees has to be felt to be appreciated; even the short walk from the house to the tower is enough to freeze whatever part of your face is exposed to the knifelike wind. The winter gales wash the salty spray across the island, coating the dwellings and walkways. One morning I had to use a hammer and a screwdriver to chip away the inch-thick layer of ice which had formed on the lighthouse door. In snowstorms, the drifts cover the helicopter pad and fill the basement entryway, necessitating frequent trips outside with a snow shovel in hand. In the early part of January 1991, I shovelled a path from the lighthouse yard to the north point of the island — some 300 metres in two feet of snow. But the snow usually doesn't stay deep, because powerful winter winds will scour the island clean.

And then suddenly its spring, as the grass turns green and the first puffins and Razorbills begin to arrive on the water. The fog returns and days are passed under the foghorn's moan in a tiny world of indistinct shapes and insidious damp. It has been this way on Machias Seal Island for as long as anyone can remember, and although the fog can be constant, wet and miserable, the island just wouldn't be the same without it.

Gannet Rock, 1991. *Chris Mills photo.*

SIX
Gannet Rock:
The Rock

> I was out there for three years and if I had my choice I'd do
> it over. They were the best years I had.
>
> Doug Daggett, Principal Keeper on
> Gannet Rock, 1971-74[26]

GANNET ROCK is one of the few truly isolated rock stations in
the Maritimes and probably comes closest to the archetypal
tower rising out of the sea found in popular stories of
shipwrecks. Gannet's tower is all the more noteworthy because
of its construction: with the exception of a granite and concrete
base, it is built entirely of wood. That the tower has lasted
through 160 years of storm and tide is a tribute to its builders,
who worked under less than ideal conditions with simple tools,
blasting and moving stone and timber to build the massive
wooden-beamed structure. Ironically, the birds for which the
rock was named disappeared with the construction of the
lighthouse. It was the only nesting ground in the area and,
although today the large birds are visible in the summer and
fall, diving for fish in the turbulent waters around the rock, the
nearest breeding colony is on the appropriately named Bird
Rocks in the Gulf of St. Lawrence.

Today, Gannet Rock is one of the few remaining wooden

colonial towers in the Bay of Fundy area that remains relatively intact, and it is the second oldest wooden lighthouse still in use in Canada. It is also one of the very few lighthouses in the Maritimes with resident lightkeepers. Although the tasks performed by the present-day guardians have changed since the first days of lightkeeping on the rock, the tradition has continued, despite the looming threat of full automation. When keeper Captain Lamb lit the light for the first time on Christmas Eve in 1831, though, automation was undoubtedly the furthest thing from his mind. Lamb's job was crucial to the safety of ships entering and leaving the Bay of Fundy, and he performed his tasks diligently until opting for transfer to the relatively urban Quaco lighthouse near St. Martin's. He was succeeded by a Mr. Miller who, along with his assistant, drowned in 1837.

The man whose name is now synonymous with Gannet Rock began work at age sixteen as an assistant to his brother Henry in 1845. Walter B. McLaughlin spent a total of thirty-five years as a keeper on the rock, leaving in 1880 to assume duties at the newly established Southwest Head light. McLaughlin was the quintessential lightkeeper — a philosopher, poet and diarist — a man well suited to the ascetic life of Gannet Rock. His legacy, a set of detailed journals, remains to this day, a valuable record of life and times on an isolated rock. His lighthouse diaries carefully detail storms, shipwrecks, tides, wind, wildlife and atmospheric phenomena.

In his splendid isolation, McLaughlin witnessed and recorded awesome displays of northern lights, earth tremors, the arrival of the first land birds each spring, winds and waves that repeatedly ripped up the station's decking, and great fires on Grand Manan. In October 1871 he recorded seeing great clouds of smoke pass over the rock and declared that a large American city was burning. During a visit of the supply boat some time later, McLaughlin learned of the Great Chicago Fire. One hundred twenty years later, from the lantern deck of the tower on Gannet Rock, I saw the pall of smoke over Grand

Walter B. McLaughlin on his 50th wedding anniversary, January 11, 1905. *Grand Manan Museum*.

Manan from a massive forest fire on the north shore of the St. Lawrence River.

Despite its physical isolation, the rock has been a convenient spot from which to observe both natural and human history. In 1895, Joshua Slocum passed Gannet Rock at the beginning of his famous journey around the world. On September 28, 1936, the zeppelin *Von Hindenburg* was plainly visible at eight p.m. proceeding westward, its progress duly noted by the lightkeeper on duty. Countless hurricanes swept up the Bay of Fundy while keepers secured the shutters and waited out the tempest. During the summer of 1984, "some sort of a twister" hit the station and winds of 115 knots pulled one of the tower's guy wires from its cement base and broke a fog detector covering. A constant stream of tankers, freighters, ocean liners, barges, oil rigs, yachts and fishing boats has passed the station, day and night. In McLaughlin's time the rock was often visited by Pleasant Point Indians, who stopped to repair their canoes after paddling from Maine across unforgiving seas.

The logs kept by McLaughlin and his successors record everything from the day's weather to visits by government administrators. Logbooks dating to the late 1920s at the station provide an invaluable record of life on the rock in the days before automation. Most entries in the "Engine Room Diary," "Lighthouse Diary," "Return of Stores" record and "Fog Signal Operating Report" are dry and factual, noting fog-alarm compressor running times, the duration of operation of the light and how many gallons of paint were used in maintenance of the station. Nevertheless, other more personal and historical information is scrawled or written in a clear, firm hand on grimy margins and covers of the books: the names of the steady stream of assistant keepers hired by the principal keeper, the lyrics of popular songs, notations of ham radio contacts, and shipwrecks. For example, on October 7, 1933, the schooner *Edna Parsons* was "upset, all lost"; bad weather in December of the same year evoked the comment

"Blowing like H" in the margin; and June 28, 1943, brought a "Heavy Tempest" to the rock.

Damage from storms was a fact of life for keepers. In 1845, Walter McLaughlin helped to construct a granite retaining wall around the station following a particularly violent gale three years earlier. Almost a century later, on September 15, 1944, a "very heavy storm destroyed wharf, broke end in on oil shed, side in cookhouse, broke windows in house, washed ammunition shed away." As if that wasn't enough, on February 16, 1953, the railings on the wharf were broken, and the sea broke in the main entry door. Solid water broke open the whistlehouse doors and washed away half the boards on the west wall, and flooded the kitchen.

Over the years the kitchen seems to have received more than its fair share of storm damage, and reports of cookstoves being moved around the room were fairly common until recently. The most recent storm to do major damage on Gannet was in 1976, when the Groundhog Day gale pummelled New Brunswick and the southern shore of Nova Scotia. Principal Keeper Don Denton and assistant Ashton Fleet watched helplessly as massive waves driven by a wind peaking at 130 knots smashed into the dwelling, breaking windows in the kitchen and flooding the ground floor of the structure. As the men stood in the swirling waters of the kitchen, they noticed that the sink was full of water as well, and that the radio which had previously sat on the shelf above the counter was now floating in the sink, with music playing, no less! Contact with the mainland was broken and with both stoves downstairs extinguished, the keepers were without heat for six long hours. From the top of the lighthouse the concrete deck surrounding the station was invisible, hidden in a furious cascade of breaking seas. Some people on Grand Manan said Gannet Rock wouldn't even be there after the storm, but the 145-year-old tower and its inhabitants managed to survive the blow.

The logs have also recorded the tedium of lightstation life:

Ice formed by freezing spray on rock, station seawall and tower guy wires. *Chris Mills photos.*

painting, oil changes, weather reports, cleaning, scrubbing and more painting. In 1974, new automated generators were installed, but throughout that and the next year, log entries recorded troubles with the new system. In recent years the station records have become increasingly domestic in nature as the maintenance of most equipment has passed from the hands of the keepers to mechanics and technicians.

In the early days of Gannet's history, the lightkeepers lived on the rock with their families; Walter McLaughlin brought his bride to the lighthouse in 1855. No records of Mrs. McLaughlin's observations of life on Gannet Rock are known to exist, but one can imagine that life for a married couple on such a small site would pose special difficulties. As late as 1931, wives and children lived on the rock, and the wife of one keeper in the 1920s stated that she had enjoyed life on Gannet despite being separated from friends and family.

In 1898, Lincoln Harvey brought his family to the rock and his daughter remembers the huge wooden-beamed house and a storm that flooded the dwelling and moved the great iron stove around the kitchen. By the 1950s, keepers were working month-long shifts on the rock without their families and spending off-duty time ashore. In recent years Gannet has been a mens' domain, although in the late 1980s a husband and wife team spent at least two shifts on the station.

The lives of lightkeepers have been revolutionized by modern communications and helicopters, to say nothing of automation, but some aspects of the job have remained unchanged. The routine and isolation of places like Gannet Rock has always been an integral part of a keeper's experience. Regular watch duties have set the pace for countless shifts, and extra time has been whiled away woodcarving, fishing, painting and, more recently, watching TV. Many traditional lighthouse duties have disappeared in just the last twenty years. There is no longer the huge second-order lens to polish, nor the compressors to start up at the sight of fog. Engine overhauls, oil changes and repairs have ceased to be the keepers' domain in times of technological advance.

Although boredom and routine make lightkeeping in the 1990s difficult, the most unpleasant part of the whole process is the waiting: waiting to hear how much longer the station will be staffed and wondering where you will go next. Many keepers say this has been the hardest part of their job in the past two decades. No one person or group of people can be blamed for what is happening on the lights. This is a change that is occurring worldwide with lighthouses, industry and government services. Automation, destaffing and consolidation is a dehumanizing process, but it is also part and parcel of progress and technological advance.

Despite the threat of imminent destaffing, I jumped at the chance to work on Gannet Rock when a position became available. The rock had intrigued me since I had read about it in a lighthouse book in the 1970s, and I was excited when the opportunity to work a shift there presented itself. During my time on Seal and Machias Seal islands I had thought a lot about the rock and asked most of the Coast Guard technicians I met about the place. I think the general consensus was that I was crazy to even think about going near the place; it is not a favourite with the work crews who sometimes spend several weeks at a time on the station. On one occasion I spoke with a keeper on Gannet Rock from Seal Island by radio and even he told me that the best way to see Gannet Rock was from a helicopter — on the way home! Nevertheless, on a cold February day in 1991, I unloaded my gear from the chopper and stared up at the great wooden tower for the first time.

In the end I spent a total of five months on the rock. I came to love the place, despite its sometimes claustrophobic atmosphere. There was something special about the black and white, vertically striped tower in the middle of the sea. The smell of saltwater and diesel and the sound of the foghorn on days when you couldn't see your hand in front of your face created a compelling atmosphere difficult to resist. I knew this even before I had finished unloading my gear on that windy February day.

(Above) From glass plate photo, taken around the turn of the century — before tower heightened and new lantern and lens installed. *Grand Manan Museum*. (Below) "Riding the rails" at Gannet Rock on the way down to the lifeboat of Wood Island Lifesaving Station, which has arrived at the rock with a load of water and supplies. Circa 1930. *Grand Manan Museum*.

My immediate impression was that this was a place out of time. The tattered half of a Coast Guard flag strained on the flagpole and, outside the huge black and white tower, a clutter of equipment lay strewn on the deck. At the top of the old tramway in front of the main entrance sat a rust-streaked grey and red cart with a single davit, used at one time to launch the station dory which now lies strapped to the cement deck below the tower. It's not too seaworthy now, and a keeper with a sense of humour has painted "Coast Guard Flower Pot" in spidery letters on the bow.

Attached to the southern side of the tower stands a stark two-storey concrete dwelling with blank windows, some shuttered and some not. The place is weather worn and yet sturdy, like an old pickup truck that still runs OK. The old whistlehouse, demolished in part to make way for a fuel bunker, resembles a ruined castle with tall grey walls against the sea. From seaward, and from Grand Manan, Gannet Rock appears as a fortress with ramparts set against an otherwise unbroken horizon.

The house is reached by a set of doors that lead from the base of the tower to the living room. On the east and west sides are bedrooms, and to the south the kitchen. The living room is small and brightly lit by a naked 100-watt blub hanging from the ceiling. The room is filled with furniture and equipment: a small bookshelf stuffed with westerns and war stories, a large two-burner Enterprise heater in front of a small mantlepiece, a coffee table in front of a double window, wall to wall carpet on the floor. Next to the TV sits a big blue metal box containing the lighthouse link with Yarmouth Coast Guard radio in Nova Scotia. A bulletin board above the radio displays a "Be Alert and Live Around the Helicopter" poster, as well as a tide table and several official memos concerning lighthouse logbooks, unsafe emergency light towers, and annual holidays.

The mercury barometer is mounted near the west bedroom door, next to a Bank of Nova Scotia calendar. On the wall are associated charts, a barograph, wind indicators and the fishermen's VHF radio, busy with talk of trawls, quotas and weather conditions. Over the door to the tower a lone speaker pipes in more static from another VHF radio upstairs — an endless stream of Coast Guard weather reports, ship traffic, monitoring stations and Yarmouth Coast Guard radio. Outside the east-facing living room windows is no green lawn or blacktop driveway, but a cement deck, bordered by red and white railings, and beyond that the expanse of sea and sky.

Through the southern doorway is the kitchen, with its bright white and aquamarine walls, fridge, deep-freeze and Kemac cookstove. An aluminum painted stovepipe runs north across the ceiling after twisting its way out of the stove to join the pipe from the living room heater. The back entryway has steps which lead upstairs to an identical apartment, only this time with a bathroom in place of one bedroom. A door on the north wall of the living-room wall leads to the tower's second floor and, turning left, one can climb the remaining stairs past the four landings to the lantern.

The tower is guyed with heavy cables to protect it from the extreme force of high winds. From the lantern deck the view is superb, and when one steps back from the edge it appears that the tower stands alone in the sea. On a clear night, thirteen lighthouses can be seen from the lantern deck, including Petit Manan some thirty nautical miles to the westward in Maine and Cape Forchu in Nova Scotia, more than fifty miles to the southeast. Below the lantern everything is close: tower, house, horn, helipad, wharf, rocks and sea. The station is old, a labyrinth of rooms and passageways, filled with old tools, windows, panel doors, oil stoves, hardwood floors and plaster walls.

In some ways it is like a ship, with the lantern as the bridge and the tower and house as superstructure and afterdeck, respectively. The continuous rumble of the diesels, the traffic on VHF radios, and the endless swell rolling by creates the illusion that the rock is moving slowly and steadily over the sea. The smells of cigarettes, diesel fuel and cooking add to the deception.

The tower has seven floors, including the lantern; eighty-

Chris Mills — baker deluxe.

six steps lead to the top. From the base of the tower a wooden stairway leads around the corner of the engine room up to the second floor, which contains supplies, water tanks and a separate small room for the foghorn and automation equipment. The fog detector is located on the western face of the tower, halfway between the first and second floors along the stairway. Past the door to the second floor of the dwelling, the stairway continues its course upward, past four more landings to the lantern. Balustrades and railings are painted red, as are the centres of the stair treads, and the rest is grey. The upper part of the tower is panelled with matched lumber painted light yellow.

On the third and fourth floors are small rooms off the landings with remnants of laths and plaster clinging to wall studs. These rooms were once lived in by the keepers and their families, and when you enter, you can feel the age of the tower. One keeper has written his name and the stations where he had served on the wall of the third-floor room: Cape North, Cape Roseway, Cape Sable, Gannet Rock. The fourth-floor room has a small door which leads out to the foghorn platform on the southern exposure of the tower. Through the centre of the tower runs a conduit that carries power to the main light. This conduit follows the path of the original weight tube that was used until an electric motor replaced the clockwork mechanism that rotated the massive lens.

The large circular iron lantern and second-order Fresnel lens were removed in 1967 and replaced with a simple rotating airport beacon housed in an aluminum lantern. The 1904-vintage lantern and lens were removed after doubts arose about the structural integrity of the tower as a support for the multi-ton apparatus. As the tedious process of removing the lens piece by piece began, it became evident that the structure was very much intact. The lantern itself was so firmly attached to the tower that it had to be hauled off by attaching a cable to the Coast Guard ship *Thomas Carleton*. The *Carleton* pulled the lantern completely off the tower and it landed in a gully on the western side of the rock. Its remains are visible to this day

— heavy chunks of shattered, ornate ironwork. Pieces of the iron railings and grillwork are washed by the tides as they rust into obscurity. Crevices and cracks all around Gannet Rock are filled with reminders of the station's past: huge flywheels from steam and single-cylinder gas engines, boiler plates, copper wire, pipes, valves, cylinder heads, crankshafts, turnbuckles, shackles, pistons and water tanks. The mechanical history of the lightstation is scattered around its perimeter, as decaying reminders of the days of spotless engine rooms and gleaming brasswork. In the rock itself are dozens of iron eyes and rods, protruding from the conglomerate. Many were mooring rings from the days when ships and barges brought regular shipments of coal, water and oil. And, over the years, several men have carved their names and initials on railings, rampways and in the rock itself.

Arrival on any lightstation, whether for the first time or the twentieth, is an interesting experience. An introduction to Gannet Rock is no exception. From the southeast, the rock appears to be so small that is is hard to believe that there is room for two people, let alone a helicopter. On the final approach, the chopper noses up into the wind and carefully sets down on the twenty-six-foot-square wooden pad. The keepers pile out and begin unloading supplies. From the helicopter pad (which is more like a wharf on the north end of the rock), a short ramp leads to the main deck around the tower and the keepers' dwelling. On the east side of the tower, the main entryway leads to the engine room at the base of the light and to the dwelling.

Boxes, cartons and duffel bags are hastily carried inside while the chopper idles on the pad, its blades cutting the air. As the departing keepers close the helicopter doors and wave goodbye, the new shift begins the process of settling in. It takes most of the day to unpack twenty-eight days worth of provisions and to set up sleeping quarters. Then there is the news to catch up on: how did your partner make out with such and such a project while he was ashore, and how is that old truck running now? Then time is spent taking a quick look at the previous shift's log entries and around the station to see if anything has changed. Usually nothing has and you settle in for the duration.

Unless specific tasks need to be performed, your time is essentially your own. Weather reports punctuate the day at three-hour intervals, and contact with Coast Guard radio regularly puts keepers in touch with the mainland. Calls for local weather conditions from fishermen around Grand Manan come in at all hours, and my partner and I took turns at the early watch to man the VHF. Nevertheless, aside from the weather and radio work, we were basically free to do what we wished. I spent as much time as possible outside, clambering over the rocks, photographing and videotaping the station and its surroundings from every angle.

I painted railings, fuel-line covers, window frames, and chopper-pad markings, and when I tired of painting I washed windows, fog-detector lenses and the lantern and main light. For exercise, I ran the hip-jarring course around the tower and dwelling, timing myself by stopwatch or by the blasts of the foghorn. My partner would walk back and forth along the cement deck, an endless march from the fuel bunker to the end of the wharf and then back again. When it wasn't fit to be outside, I'd walk up and down the tower stairs, 1,700 steps in fifteen minutes.

Inside there was always maintenance work to be done: wiping down the engines, housecleaning, servicing the desalinator, filling oil jugs for the thirsty stoves and, of course, painting. Stairs, floors, ceilings, window frames, stovepipes and oil jugs received high-gloss coats of red, white and grey, the standard lighthouse colours.

When I wasn't exercising or working on maintenance, I kept my personal lighthouse journal, reflecting on the day's activities and my feelings about lightkeeping. After almost three years on the lights, I came to the conclusion that most keepers are a bit nuts. I don't know if the profession has a tendency to attract people who are a bit offbeat or if it actually makes people that way, but over the years the lights have seen more than their fair share of interesting individuals. Some keepers have fussed about insignificant details that most people ashore wouldn't think about twice. There have been some real characters: fastidious cleaners, those who put masking tape on floors and tables to mark territory, and others who have withdrawn totally from interactions with their partners. Near murders and other animosities between keepers, after living so close for so long finally took its toll, also marked lighthouse life in the past.

In my three years as a keeper I can't recall not getting along with any of the people with whom I worked, although there were times when I needed to get away to avoid a confrontation. In most cases the issues which arise are caused by minor incidents, which ashore would seem trivial. When you spend several weeks at a time with one other person, though, even the smallest disagreement or misunderstanding can be blown out of proportion. Nevertheless, relations between keepers are usually amicable. Quite possibly there are no more crazy people on the lights than there are among any group of people, but on the lights the keepers have been left to their own devices and have flourished as "individuals."

As a matter of interest and to help pass away the time, I released several notes in bottles from the rock, as I had done earlier from Machias Seal Island. Several bottles were found, mostly in Maine, and one reply came from Cape Cod. People were interested to find them and most wrote to ask why the bottles were sent and from where. A newspaper reporter from Virginia whose friend had found a bottle in Maine called me and interviewed me about the bottles and my time on Gannet Rock. The idea of a lightkeeper on a tiny rock, obviously lonely and bored beyond belief, was appealing to this journalist.

On good days I picked dulse, a broad-bladed seaweed which grows around the rock. On several occasions I tried to dry some over the stove, but I wasn't able to achieve the fine texture and crispness that has made Grand Manan's Dark Harbour dulse famous for years. I preferred to eat mine right off the rocks anyway, enjoying the lettucelike crunch and salty taste. Seaweed is the only flora to be found around Gannet Rock, aside from the few grasses and weeds that cling to the rock and cement around the lighthouse. I planted a few sunflower seeds in some earth brought from the mainland, but they didn't survive long. The principal keeper planted potatoes in a sandy area between the helicopter pad and the lighthouse deck and harvested a very small crop in the fall. It is conceivable that a small garden could survive on Gannet Rock, but only for a short time, because winter winds and waves scour the surface clean.

In the spring and autumn, the rock is overrun with birds: sparrows, flycatchers, wrens, Mourning Doves, Bluejays, flickers, hawks, pigeons, eiders, terns, shags, guillemots, nuthatches and warblers. During foggy conditions many birds were attracted to the revolving light and flew around the lantern, like moths around a candle. Many were killed by flying into the glass and it was not unusual to find twenty or thirty dead flycatchers and sparrows on the deck in the morning. On other nights, hundreds of storm-petrels fluttered around the lantern; it was difficult to mistake their soft squeaks and clumsy fluttering on the lantern deck.

During autumn migration, Sharp-shinned and Marsh Hawks circle the rock, feeding on the multitudes of smaller birds who have stopped to rest. The hawks and Rusty Blackbirds also scavenge, eating the carcasses of birds that have flown into the light. Fairly recently more than 300 dead birds were picked off the deck on one morning, but in the last few years the number of casualties seems to have decreased. This may be due in part to the new main light, which is substantially smaller than the massive lens removed in 1967. In the summer, birds get into the house, and chasing them up through the tower to let them out through the lantern door becomes one of the regular chores.

It takes a while to become accustomed to the noises of a lightstation; each establishment has its own audio character. After a time the interaction of the noises you hear becomes part of an instinctual pattern that puts you in tune with the running of the station. On Gannet the dominant sound is the diesel-powered generator that sits only three doors away from the living quarters. As the fridge cuts in and out and electric appliances are used, the sound of the generator changes frequency. When I was outside I could always tell when my partner was using the toaster — the sound of the diesel's exhaust deepened and black smoke blew from the pipe.

On Gannet Rock things run at a certain tempo, and when this tempo is altered you notice the change almost immediately. During my last shift, one of the generators almost went down on low voltage and I noticed the different sound of the engine right away. I have always wondered how, in the days when keepers kept their watches in engine rooms, they could sleep through the deafening sounds of the machinery and foghorn. Most old-time keepers said they could take naps when the equipment was operating properly, but they would awaken immediately when an engine skipped a beat or the horn stopped blowing. To some extent this instinct applies today. On Gannet, when the foghorn is on, you don't hear it after a while, even though it is right over the house. Some nights we'd be sitting watching TV and one of us would say "Hey, has the horn stopped?" We'd both listen, and sure enough the stovepipe would buzz and the window would rattle with the next three blasts.

This "instinct" reinforced by routine also applies to the environment around the station. One night during the summer, I took a quick stroll in the back courtyard before turning in. Looking westward, I noticed immediately that the light on Machias Seal Island was out. I had been so accustomed to seeing its bright flash on the horizon that I knew immediately that something was different. The next day I found that the generators had been down and the light had been out for several hours.

There were other noises on the station to which I became accustomed. The kitchen stove made a low roar and behind it was the bubbling sound of the oil in the jug. The fridge always cut in with a raucus buzz (one noise that never failed to startle me even after five months on the station.) There was always the chatter on the VHF radios, country music on AM radio and, in the evenings, the murmur of news and sitcoms on TV. During rough weather, especially when we had a big swell from the south, the constant battering of the surf was percussive and literally shook the rock. In rainstorms the weather beat a steady tattoo on the windows, and the splattering sound from overflowing eavestroughs echoed in the back courtyard.

Collecting and storing good quality water has always been a problem on the lights. Until 1987, drinking water on Gannet was collected from roof gutters on the dwelling, as was done on most stations, and stored in a cistern in the base of the tower. It was difficult to keep salt out of the supply because frequent winds and waves left salt deposits on the roof and in the gutters. Eventually a reverse-osmosis desalinator was installed and that continues to provide potable water for the station today. The desalinator itself seemed to work reasonably well during my time on the rock but needed constant monitoring, as dirty filters and loose fittings often caused the system to work below capacity or to leak profusely. More than once a keeper cursed eloquently as he stepped into half an inch of water on the entryway floor after having forgotten to empty the bucket under the leak.

The saltwater cistern that supplies the desalinator is pumped out with a fire pump and hose, which takes about fifteen minutes. Filling the cistern is more time-consuming and first involves wheeling a specially designed submersible pump from the base of the tower to the lower landing below the helipad. Here it is hooked up to a small derrick with a hand winch and a guide rope moored by a cement block below. A hose is attached to the upper end of the pump and, after being lowered into the water, the pump and hose are briefly flushed.

The hose is then connected to a pipeline which runs to the tower, and pumping commences. Forty-five minutes or so are needed to fill the cistern and, when this is done, everything is hauled up and stowed. Appropriate valves are opened and closed and the desalinator is started.

We usually filled the cistern every three days and, although this was a fairly routine task, it was often made uncomfortable and dangerous by the weather. During autumn and winter storms, waves washed over the lower wharf where we worked. On one occasion a large wave crashed into the landing, soaking my partner. Fortunately he shielded me from most of the wet!

Despite the fact that I've lived in rural areas for most of my life I didn't begin to take real notice of the weather until I began work as a lightkeeper. In urban areas the weather is not an integral part of people's lives, but simply an environmental variable noted mainly for the pleasure or annoyance it causes. Shovelling driveways in the winter and running errands around town in the rain are bothersome but nothing more, because they do not have a truly meaningful effect on day-to-day activities. However, if you are a farmer or a fishermen, you take careful note of the weather because it directly affects your livelihood.

On Gannet Rock you cannot help but be affected by the weather because you are so exposed to the elements. Constant calls from fishermen for weather conditions and three hourly reports for Environment Canada made us continually aware of changes in the wind and sky. In the spring and summer, the Bay of Fundy becomes a vast, fog-shrouded harbour, with hundreds of foghorns, bells, whistles and ships' sirens sounding. Invisible fishing vessels pass by the rock, feeling their way with radar. The fog is clammy, and immediate surroundings become indistinct. You are alone in a world so small that you can walk around it in a minute.

And the fog is fickle. Once when I arose early for the

morning watch, I took a quick look around outside just as the day began to break. Although it was foggy I could see five or six miles, at least. I climbed to the top of the tower for a better look around and stepped out on the lantern deck into a thick, wet fog. In the time it had taken me to climb the eighty-six steps, the visibility had dwindled to zero. When I hung out the wash on a clear and sunny day, I always kept an eye out for fog, as it can roll in unexpectedly and very quickly. When it was foggy, the wash often came in wetter than when it was hung out.

Fog was a constant companion during some shifts, showing no sign of clearing as we neared shift change day. My notes from a summer shift describe the situation:

> The fog lies in a low curtain as the black waters eddy and swirl around the exposed rocks. It is clear overhead, but in the middle of the surrounding wall of fog we might as well be looking up at the sky from the confines of a prison yard. Our fears are confirmed as the keeper on duty at Letite calls to say that the visibility in St. John is near zero and that the chopper won't be going anywhere today. Necessary items from the carefully packed gear are removed and we resign ourselves to at least one more night on the rock. Although the last week of a shift is slow, the last day is worse, as keepers do a last minute tidy up while keeping an ear tuned for the sound of the chopper or news on the VHF. Sometimes the process is like a game of cat and mouse, with the fog retreating and then shutting in again just as the chopper lifts off from the Coast Guard Base in St. John.

Sometimes you're delayed ashore too. Often I spent days at home or in Yarmouth waiting for the fog to lift and the rain to stop. It could be clear across the bay, but an impenetrable fog bank off Yarmouth could prevent the chopper from reaching us as surely as would a brick wall. At the end of a shift in August we departed Gannet Rock, dodging low, thick patches of fog until we reached Brier Island, twenty-five miles across the bay. From above, the dense stratus looked harmless, but once inside, you lost all sense of motion and direction. Each season has its own type of bad weather. In the winter, frequent storms dash spray over the rock, covering everything with a layer of ice. The lantern windows freeze, obscuring the light and we trudge up the steps to spray methyl hydrate on the glass. In the house the old stoves work full blast to keep the chill out of the concrete structure. When the wind gear freezes, frequent trips outside onto the slippery deck are necessary to check the weather. When the forecast calls for winds of forty knots or more, we close most of the wooden shutters to protect the windows from the buffeting winds and the occasional slash of spray. During a good breeze the tower stands firm, anchored to the rock by eight one-inch steel cables, but the wind roars around the eaves and tugs at the shutters.

Inside the tower the wind sounds as though it will rip shingles off the structure, and in the lantern the noise is deafening and you can feel the tower vibrating in the gusts. Occasionally shutters come loose, smashing back and forth. I awakened early one morning to a heavy pounding upstairs and found that the bathroom shutter was hanging by one hinge. As a heavy rain fell, the forty-five-knot wind playfully smashed it against the frame of the window, almost shattering the glass until it tore loose and landed not too far from where I was standing.

In the spring and summer, the tempests are relieved by endless days of fog and rain. In the spring and autumn when easterly rainstorms slash across the rock we form a bucket brigade of two in order to stem the flow of water through the old windows. I don't think there is one window in the whole dwelling that doesn't leak at all. Old cloth torn into strips is placed along the sills and rung out at regular intervals. Perhaps the most disconcerting thing about the rain is not the leaking windows but the way the water drips from the fuse box in the kitchen!

Although we had our fair share of storms during my time on the rock, we did not experience any weather out of the ordinary. During the summer 1991, when news of Hurricane Bob began to reach us, we kept track of its movement up the eastern seaboard of the USA through radio and TV reports. When it looked as though the Bay of Fundy would be hit, we began to close up the dwelling. Throughout the afternoon of August 19 we kept an eye on the wind gauge, but it was not until after midnight that the storm really picked up. I saw the wind speed go as high as sixty-five knots, about the same as any winter storm, really. Although a fair amount of spray washed over the rock, it was not solid water, as most of the wind blew during an ebb tide.

By dawn, the seas and wind had diminished. CBC Radio in Halifax called to interview me to see how we had fared during the blow. Although the storm hadn't hit us as hard as it had Massachusetts and Maine, several weirs around Grand Manan had been destroyed and at Cape Forchu, Nova Scotia, two young women had been washed off the rocks at the height of the blow. Despite an intensive search of the surrounding waters and coast, their bodies were never found.

I often found it difficult to sleep during storms. Although I never felt unsafe on the rock during rough weather, I preferred to remain awake so that I could keep an eye on the equipment and the leaking windows. I'd make several trips up the tower throughout the evening and the wee hours, noting changes in the speed and direction of the wind and mopping up leaks in the old structure as it creaked and groaned around me.

In contrast, despite its often tempestuous weather, Gannet Rock can be a tranquil spot at times. My journal records the sights and smells of windless summer days:

On rare calm days, at the edge of the rocks at low tide the mainland looks to be only a stone's throw away. When there is no wind, the sun bakes the rock and the smell of salt and drying seaweed is strong in the air. It's hard to escape the staccato beat of the lighthouse engine, but on a hot day it adds to the intensity of the feeling. Grand Manan shimmers in the distance and to the west the Murr Ledges loom up like rocky crags. The surrounding rocks are covered with Herring and Great Blackbacked Gulls, preening and resting. The weed covered rocks are also convenient sunning areas for fat and lazy seals who snooze for hours in the heat of the day. Emerald pools in dripping caverns are exposed, inhabited by amphipods, crabs, starfish and sea anenomes. As the day warms, the seaweed gently steams, and the air is filled with the sharp smell of iodine.

On the station flies cover the dwelling and fill the lantern with incessant buzzing. They get into your hair and eyes and mouth and fill up sticky fly strips within a matter of hours. Coffee cups collect drowned fliers, as does the oil pan at the back of the stove. In the house it is hot, too hot, as most of the windows have been painted shut for years. The stove must stay lit most of the time to keep hot water in the tank. We open the few windows that haven't been sealed shut and the wind shifts to northwest, filling the house with the harsh fumes from the diesel exhaust.

I called Gannet on my hand-held VHF from Grand Manan during a twenty-eight-day leave once and asked what was going on and how hot was it out there anyway? The answer was that nothing too much was happening, but it was "so hot that a fella has to get up and move around once in a while just to make a breeze!"

Despite being surrounded by water and for so many years a crucial part of marine navigation, the lighthouse has in many ways turned away from the sea. Throughout the nineteenth and early twentieth centuries the only contact with lightstations on islands and on the mainland was by water. Supplies and manpower were moved by ships, tenders, rowboats, sailboats and surfboats, and then moved to the station by winch and aerial hoist. Slipways, tramways and boathouses were integral components of almost every lightstation. As the twentieth century progressed, roads linked mainland lights with communities, lessening the need to transport supplies by water. Since the mid 1970s, even island and rock stations have lost their boats — tramways have rusted, slipways have been torn up and boats have been removed or tied up. All lightkeeper reliefs are now done by helicopter, and most supplies are brought out in nets and cages instead of by ship and barge.

No longer are barrels and boxes loaded and offloaded laboriously by hand. Now the chopper slings loads of sand, cement, shingles, tarpaper, tar, nails, toilet paper, blankets, sleeping bags, folding beds, aluminum towers, plywood, two-by-fours, paint, grout, electrical wiring and ladders. Fuel-oil delivery, although still from a ship, is made by a chopper slinging 150-gallon fuel bladders that are set on chopper pads and pumped into station tanks.

On Gannet Rock we are surrounded by the sea and affected by it but have no real interaction with it. As lightkeepers we are less and less an integral part of the marine environment, and more and more simply spectators. Although a large amount of marine activity occurs around the rock, especially during lobster season, few visits are made by fishermen. Nowadays the rock sees very few people other than Coast Guard personnel. We did have one special visit, though, the first of its kind in many years. Ernest "Rip" Irwin is a good friend of mine, and a fellow lighthouse enthusiast. For the past five years we have visited several lights in the Maritimes, and Rip's purchase of a Zodiac and outboard has made it possible for him to visit many isolated lights along Nova Scotia's eastern and southern shores.

With a view to visiting Gannet Rock while I was on duty,

(Above) Waiting to launch Rip's 14' inflatable after his three-day visit.(Below) Dave Bailey, Jacques Godbout, and Dennis Malloch with Coast Guard helicopter at Gannet Rock. *Chris Mills photos.*

Rip came to Grand Manan with his fourteen-foot inflatable Zodiac and made preparations to "set sail" for the rock, an eight-mile journey in dangerous waters. Inclement weather, including Hurricane Bob, caused several delays until Thursday, August 22, when the fog cleared somewhat and the sea went down. Conditions were not great in the morning but were the best they had been in several days. By mid-morning the fog was thicker than ever. At 1000 hours Rip called the station on his hand-held VHF and informed us that he had just arrived at the Seal Cove Fairway buoy (some three miles from Seal Cove) and was changing his course for Gannet Rock. I kept a watch from the tower and the lower landing with binoculars and portable radio at hand, but it was nearly impossible to see anything in the dense, grey murk. It seemed highly unlikely that he could find our tiny rock without the assistance of radar or loran. Finally, three hours after my last contact with Rip, I looked up from my perch on the lower landing to see a tiny rubber craft with an orange-jacketed figure at the helm approaching from the south! Although he had overshot the rock by half a mile or so as a result of the ebb tide, he had been able to pick up the sound of our horn and correct his course.

So he'd made it, eight miles in thick fog, with only a hand compass, wristwatch and chart. By the time Rip had left Grand Manan, it seemed that most of the island knew of his plans — half thought he was crazy and the other half thought he wouldn't make it. That evening we received a call on the radio for our weather conditions; after I reported the wind speed and direction, the caller enquired, "By the way, did you happen to get a visitor today?" When he found that Rip had arrived safely, he seemed relieved and said that people had been wondering "how the fellow made out."

Finding the rock in thick fog hadn't been the only difficult task. Landings on Gannet are notoriously difficult, and this day was no exception. There is only one landing site, and it is located at the bottom of the old cement and steel tramway, halfway along a gully which runs along the east side of the rock. In recent years it has fallen into disrepair; around the bottom, jagged pieces of rusted metal and old bolts jut out, ready to tear at the fabric of any Zodiac that ventures too close. The situation is made worse by the surge of water through the gut, which increases as the tide rises. Getting Rip and the boat onto the rocks next to the haul-up was a risky task, especially with only one person ashore. A couple of large surges soaked me and brought the boat close to the jagged metal. At one point we were unable to control the craft and it hit the side of the haul-up, making a sound like a blowing whale. Immediately the port side of the boat lost all its air and then the craft began to turn around so the starboard side was in danger. With supreme effort we were able to haul the Zodiac up onto the rocks. There had been a few tense moments and we were both relieved to have the boat and Rip ashore. He ended up staying on the rock for two nights and was able to leave three days after his arrival, having repaired the hole with a temporary patch, much like the Pleasant Point Indians who had repaired their canoes on the rock more than a century before.

During my time on the rock we also had visits from other lightkeepers. In the summer we had heard news that St. Paul Island in Cape Breton would be closing, as would the lighthouse-monitoring station at Eddy Point, near Mulgrave. In early August the keepers arrived on the big Bell helicopter from the Dartmouth Coast Guard base to look around the station and then flew off to see Machias Seal Island. In October a twenty-three-year veteran of the Great Lakes lights arrived on Gannet Rock to look the station over. By the end of that month, one keeper had decided to take the position left by a retiring keeper on Machias, and in November Peter Coletti, from the recently automated Southeast Shoal light in Lake Erie landed on Gannet Rock for his first shift — quite a change for him from the freshwater lights of the Great Lakes.

Other visitors arrived too, some from Environment

Canada or Telecom, Coast Guard construction workers, mechanics and electronics technicians and very occasionally supervisory staff from the Coast Guard in Saint John and regional headquarters. Some had been to the station many times; others who were seeing the place for the first time marvelled at the size and location of the establishment and at the keepers' ability to remain sane while in such isolation. How could I explain that I felt comfortable in such a place? I didn't attempt to, and usually agreed that I was perhaps a "few bricks short of a load" after spending three years on the lights.

On December 24, 1991, Gannet Rock celebrated its 160th anniversary without fanfare. The keepers went about their business as they have done on previous anniversaries: ashore their families prepared to celebrate Christmas. It has been the same on the rock throughout the years: some keepers have celebrated the day and others have purposely ignored the occasion so the day is like any other. My final shift ended some time before Christmas, though, and on the twenty-third of October I packed up my gear and climbed into the chopper for a final trip ashore. After refuelling at Southwest Head on Grand Manan, we flew back to Yarmouth, passing once again over Gannet. As we left the rock behind I thought of the generations of men and women who had made the place home, and I remembered a poem written by Forest Wilcox of Deep Cove, Grand Manan, a retired keeper who spent eight years of his life tending the lonely beacon:

A Lightkeeper's Dream

While keeping watch down here last night
The weather being fine
I thought I'd have a little nap
To pass away the time.

I put my feet up on the stove
And soon began to snore

I dreamed I'd left the vale of tears
And reached that golden shore.

St. Peter met me at the gate
And said "Come in my lad.
Your record while you were on earth
It sure looks mighty bad.

But as you have served time on Gannet Rock
One thing I surely know,
You could get no greater punishment
If I sent you down below.

See over there on yonder point
There stands a golden light
You will never have to tend it
For up here there is no night.

No rain, no vapour, fog or snow
In this fair land you'll never see
And you can play with mermaids on the beach
Through all eternity."

My! What a wondrous time I had
Upon that golden beach
But the little mermaids in the sea
Stayed just beyond my reach.

Just then my feet fell off the stove
It was a dreadful shock
To wake and find that I was still
Right here on Gannet Rock.

When my time does come to go
And leave this world behind
When I reach that golden gate
I hope that Pete doesn't change his mind.

But give me the golden light
Beside a peaceful sea

And I hope those mermaids in the surf
Will be waiting there for me.

Undated. *Grand Manan Museum.*

Epilogue

BY THE time I had finished writing this book, four more lighthouses in the Maritimes had succumbed to the restless advance of automation, including two of the stations on which I had worked. Two others were slated for full automation by 1993, leaving Machias Seal Island and Gannet Rock as the sole beacons still under human supervision; anachronistic reminders of a way of life so integral to the history of the Maritimes.

I returned to Cross Island in September 1989 as Hurricane Gabriel's huge swell smashed into the island. George and I ventured out in his open duck boat across a heaving sea in strangely windless conditions. The storm had passed 300 nautical miles south of Sable Island, and although the swell had reached us, the wind had not. The northern harbour entrance, a narrow gut between the main island and Little Cross Island was almost impossible to enter as the seas washed through. Seaweed and debris stirred up by the swell fouled the propeller as we attempted to make the harbour entrance and we drifted uncomfortably close to the crashing surf. Once inside the protective arm of the harbour, we were safe, although the outside swell created a slow and powerful wash in the harbour.

In the evening, as we sat in the cosy cabin on Clyde Spindler's boat, we saw flares to the east. The next day we heard that two people had been washed off the rocks at Gill Cove, near Ketch Harbour at the approaches to Halifax Harbour. Near midnight, as the tide rose, the slow ebb and flow of the water under our boat became more pronounced, finally snapping a couple of its mooring lines.

During the day we had walked around the island, stopping at the lightstation in the later afternoon. The lawn, overgrown with weeds, had looked as though it had never seen a mower blade. Salt spray from the seas crashing into the cliffs below the light had set off the foghorn — as it blasted into the blue sky we walked around the boarded-up houses. Along the lighthouse road the first signs of neglect were showing: the rain had washed miniature ravines in the crushed shale and the weeds and grass were beginning to encroach. It was sad to see the station abandoned, but in a way it felt as though we had never been there.

On October 17, 1990, at 0730 hours, lightkeeper James Nickerson radioed the last weather report from Seal Island to Yarmouth Coast Guard Radio. Acting Principal Keeper Brian Stoddard had departed by chopper the day before, leaving the husband of Mary Hichens' great-grand-niece to finish duties at the lighthouse for the last time ever. By early 1992 the keepers' dwelling had been torn down and the foundation prepared for the installation of fuel tanks for the automated generators. Our carefully built fence still stands, but the sheep are once again free to roam the grounds and crop what remains of the lawns.

Not long before the *Fermont* ran aground on the east side, an autumn storm hit the island, pummelling the shoreline with huge waves formed by strong northeasterly winds. At East Side, the protective breakwater below the boathouse was completely demolished by the sea, leaving the slipway to be filled in with sand and rock. With so few fishermen working from the island now, it is doubtful that the breakwater will be rebuilt. Farther to the north, some of the grassy bluff at Head Yard was washed away, and Doug Symonds told me that much of the trail leading to Race Point, at the north tip of the island, was impassable. In many places trees had been washed over the banks, and large rocks were thrown up on the grass by the immense power of the sea.

On Machias Seal Island, life has gone on as usual, alternating between summer's frenzy of birds and visitors and winter's solitude. Several months after my second shift on the station the east-facing foghorn was removed from its perch and placed with the other horn, pointing away from the house. The keepers say when they are in the house now they don't even notice the horn is on, a far cry from the ear-numbing blasts of past summers!

Barna Norton and his band of nationalists continue to raise the flag once a year, claiming U.S. sovereignty over the home of the terns and puffins. The keepers look on, as always.

And finally, Gannet Rock: as I write this I am once more sitting at the kitchen table, below the revolving light and the blasting horn, while the kettle puffs steam atop the stove lids. When I left the rock in October 1991, I had not planned to return, hoping to find work ashore. Three months later I was drawn back to the Bay of Fundy by a combination of financial necessity and love of the lights. During the summer the station had received a reprieve in the form of a memo from Ottawa which stated that the plans to destaff the lighthouse were again on hold until further notice. Nonetheless, the station's future continues to be uncertain and life on the rock is still very much a month-by-month affair.

The January-February 1992 shift was the stormiest I had seen on any of the islands. We were confined to the house for a good part of the twenty-eight days, as high winds, massive seas and sub-zero temperatures covered the windows and decks with ice. We had to hack close to six inches of ice from the lower landing in order to rig up the submersible pump for the saltwater cistern. At the end of January, two days of strong southerly winds built big seas that sent heavy spray over the southern end of the rock. On the top of the fuel bunker, some thirty-five feet above the sea, I was soaked by spray flying over the cement walls as I videotaped the maelstrom. I stopped the camera for a moment and the biggest sea of all hit, sending a wall of water between the bunker and the dwelling. The west-facing back door was smashed open, and brooms, mops and buckets scattered all over the flooded floor.

The next shift will probably see calmer weather on the rock, as the gales of winter give way to the fog and rain of spring. By April the lobster boats will be back, hauling traps marked by brightly coloured buoys and the land birds will arrive — swallows, sparrows, flycatchers and hawks. It is difficult to say how much longer I will stay here. It is doubtful that keepers will continue to return to Gannet Rock for their twenty-eight-day vigils much longer. For the moment though, the routine continues, and despite the isolation and the looming destaffing, it has been a wonderful experience for me. As the westerly breeze freshens at dusk and our light beams into the gathering dark, I know that it has all been worthwhile.

NOTES

1. Hugh F. Pullen, *The Sea Road to Halifax* (Halifax: Nova Scotia Museum, 1980), p. 22.

2. This reed horn was designed by an American, Mr. C.L. Daboll. Originally horses powered the compressor; later it was operated by Ericcson's caloric engine. The horn proved to be fairly unreliable and was not used widely for any significant period of time in North America.

3. I have often pondered the Coast Guard's mandate regarding the staffing of lighthouses, especially in these days of accurate electronic navigation through satnav and loran. With the introduction of semi-automation in the 1970s it was stressed that lighthouses would not remain staffed so keepers could render assistance to mariners in distress, as this was not part of their official duties. The official duties of a lightkeeper, it was stated, were to maintain the station grounds, observe the operation of the light and fog signal and to report any abnormalities in their operation to the Coast Guard. Although technically this was true, lightkeepers were also in a position to assist mariners in distress, and if someone got into trouble, how could they refuse to help?

Although I did not participate in any lifesaving rescues during my time as a keeper, I became well aware of the assistance given by keepers and their families up to the 1980s. Lightkeepers have always been close to areas of marine activity and many mariners have felt comfortable knowing that they could get help from, or through, lightkeepers if necessary. On Cross, Mosher's, Sambro and Whitehead islands, to name a few, keepers provided warmth and shelter to lost pleasure boaters, fixed broken-down engines, rescued boaters from capsized vessels and towed disabled boats to safety, almost right up to the time of their destaffing.

The importance of lightkeeper involvement in search and rescue was illustrated in one incident which occurred while I worked on Cross Island. One afternoon at our regular radio schedule time, the marine operator at Halifax Coast Guard Radio informed us that an ELT (emergency locator transmitter) signal had been picked up from the vicinity of Cross Island, and could we attempt to get a visual fix on the boat in trouble? I headed down the southwest shore on a four-wheeler while my partner took the skiff out around the northern end of the island. We did locate a styrofoam-encased transmitter on the west side of the island, but upon closer inspection it turned out to be part of a weather balloon.

In the meantime the Coast Guard rescue cutter based in Sambro had been dispatched, with instructions that they should meet us at the eastern entrance of our harbour and that we should assist them in the search for the elusive ELT. We were unable to find any evidence of the device and found later that the signal had come from a vessel berthed in Lunenburg! Apparently it had been dislodged by a careless painter working aboard the vessel. Although the whole episode had been a wild goose chase, it illustrated how important a presence on lightstations could still be. Nonetheless, government policy stresses that lightkeepers should have little or no direct involvement in search and rescue, and that any action taken by keepers is on a purely voluntary basis and is not condoned by the Coast Guard in any way.

4. The first steam fog whistle in British North America was put into operation on Partridge Island in Saint John Harbour in 1860. Developed by Scottish-born civil engineer Robert Foulis, this whistle was used on many Canadian lightstations until the introduction of the powerful diaphone.

5. The diaphone is a Canadian invention. It was developed in 1902 by J.P. Northey, a Toronto manufacturer, and in the first decade of the twentieth century it replaced many lower-power foghorns and whistles on Canadian lightstations. Northey's fog signal was more efficient than the popular siren developed in Britain and used extensively around the world. In the diaphone, compressed air passing through a perforated reciprocating piston assembly produced a very powerful low frequency sound which, under ideal

conditions, could be heard for more than twenty miles. Wickerson Lent, assistant keeper at the Brier Island lighthouse in the 1960s and 1970s, told me that on one occasion a fishing vessel had picked up the diaphone at this station from a distance of forty miles. By the late 1970s most diaphones had been replaced by the smaller "Airchime" horn, also developed in Canada, and by electronic horns manufactured in Great Britain and Sweden.

6. Ruth Smith, *The Smith Who Jumped Ship* (Lunenburg, 1983).

7. Provincial Archives of Nova Scotia (hereafter PANS), MG 100, vol. 127, no. 24.

8. Ibid.

9. PANS, St. John's Anglican Church Records, Book Five.

10. Ruth Smith, *The Smith Who Jumped Ship.*

11. PANS, RG 5, Series P, vol. 41, nos. 48 and 75.

12. *The Novascotian*, Halifax, December 26, 1834.

13. Ibid., October 3, 1839.

14. Ruth Smith, *The Smith Who Jumped Ship.*

15. Grace Darling is perhaps the most famous of lighthouse women, well known for her role in the rescue of five crewmembers from the steamship *Forfashire* in 1838. Ida Lewis saved at least twenty-three people from the waters of Newport Harbour, during her fifty years at the Lime Rock light.

16. In 1842, Cunard's Royal Mail steamer *Columbia* was wrecked in fog on the Black Ledges off Seal Island. The passengers and crew were saved, but the ship was lost.

17. Will R. Bird, "Nova Scotia Has Many Lights," *Canadian Geographical Journal*, March 1957.

18. A marine radio beacon was established on Seal Island in 1924. Until the late 1950s, radio operators lived on the island, maintaining the beacon and Morse code equipment; after that time, lightkeepers maintained the beacon. Until 1989 the lightkeepers were responsible for synchronizing the beacon transmissions with the standard time signal. In October 1989 a fully automatic continuous-broadcast radio beacon was installed.

19. Although the diaphone replaced many steam whistles at the

turn of the century, fog alarm buildings were still referred to as the "whistle house," a term common well into the 1980s. The buildings were also called the "fog alarm" and "engine room."

20. The Fenians were Irish-Americans with a goal of securing Irish independence from Britain in the 1860s. An American wing split into two factions, one intent in invading Canada. Raids were conducted in New Brunswick, Quebec and Manitoba. The story of the Seal Island raid was told to me by Mary Nickerson, whose mother had heard it from her mother, Caroline Crowell.

21. Although the story of the Fenian raid is difficult to verify, Seal Island's residents did suffer incursions of "marauding fishermen" from Yarmouth in the first half of the nineteenth century. In 1846, Richard Hichens wrote to Provincial Secretary Rupert George, complaining that "the loss and annoyances we meet by these people is almost beyond endurance. The last season there was more then twenty pounds worth of property taken from the Island exclusive of the loss of our sheep, many of which we find dead after the marauders leaving the island, some being shot — others mutilated and bleeding to death. So bold are some of them ... that after stealing our mooring chain from the boat establishment made their boast that we dare not board their vessel without a search warrant which they were sure could not be presented." The marauders also set fire to the grass of the island — the flames came uncomfortably close to the barn and dwelling at the lightstation.

Hichens requested that he be given authority to deal with the problem, citing past experience in dealing with unruly seafarers: "In the 10 or 12 thousand tons of Shipping that has been wrecked on this Island since my residence here, that there must have been some trouble in keeping order among so many different characters a large portion of which generally belongs to what is termed the third class of sailors — by assuming authority that I did not possess. I have often been instrumental in producing amicable settlements between Masters and men which authority I have been forced to assume to prevent blood-shed." In the interests of peace and security, Hichens was most anxious to prevent the shores of Seal Island from becoming "strewn with the corpses of Shipwrecked mariners mingled with the inhabitants of the Island in their exertions to save them."

22. Basil Small, in an interview with Hannah Gartner on "This Morning," CBC Toronto, September 8, 1976.

23. Normally one parent stays with the chick while the other brings food. When the nesting site is disturbed both parents defend

their territory, leaving the chick exposed. When the chick runs for safety into the long and often wet grass, hypothermic shock often sets in, and a chick can die after only a few minutes of exposure. Harry Thurston, Camden House, *Tidal Life: A Natural History of the Bay of Fundy* (Ottawa; 1990).

24. An International Court decision in 1953 ruled that a claim to an island because of its lighthouse had no merit. *The Saint Croix Courier*, September 23, 1987.

25. From the poem "Tall Barney," author unknown. Barna Norton sent me a copy of the fourteen-verse work.

26. *Maclean's* magazine Vol. 93, No. 4, January 28, 1980, article by David Folster.

Cape Forchu, main light, Summer 1991

SOURCE MATERIAL

Bush, Edward F., *The Canadian Lighthouse*, Canadian Historic Sites: Occasional Papers in Arcaeology and History, Ottawa, 1974.

Crowell, Edwin, *History of Barrington Township*, Mika Publishing, 1974.

Hichens, Walter W., *Island Trek*, Lancelot Press, 1982.

MacMechan, Archibald, *There Go the Ships*, McClelland and Stewart, Toronto, 1928.

Messenger, Margaret (Ed.), *Island Memories*, Archelaus Smith Historical Society, 1982.

Messenger, Margaret, *From Island to Island*, Archelaus Smith Historical Society, 1987.

Mitcham, Allison, *Offshore Islands to Nova Scotia and New Brunswick*, Lancelot Press, 1984.

Mitcham, Allison, *Paridise or Purgatory:* Island Life in Nova Scotia and New Brunswick, Lancelot Press, 1986.

Perry, Hattie A., *Mary Hichens and Her Namesake*, Hattie A. Perry, 1985.

Pullen, Rear Admiral Hugh F., *The Sea Road To Halifax:* Being an Account of the Lights and Buoys of Halifax Harbour, Nova Scotia Museum, Halifax, 1980.

Richardson, Evelyn, *We Keep a Light*, Ryerson Press, Toronto, 1961.

Richardson, Evelyn, *B was for Butter*, Petheric Press, Halifax, 1976.

Robertson, Marion, *King's Bounty:* A History of Early Shelburne Nova Scotia, Nova Scotia Museum, Halifax, 1983.

Slocum, Joshua, *Sailing Alone Around the World*, Dover Publications, 1956.

Stephens, David, *Lighthouses of Nova Scotia*, Lancelot Press, 1973.

Thurston, Harry, *Tidal Life:* A Natural History of the Bay of Fundy, Camden House, Ontario, 1990.

Whitney, Dudley, *The Lighthouse*, McClellend and Stewart, 1976.

Wickens, Sonia, *Seal Island:* An Echo from the Past, Sonia Wickens, 1988.

Canadian Geographic, Maclean's, Nova Scotia Birds, Transport Canada Lighthouse Logbooks, *The Novascotian, The Mail Star, The Chronicle Herald,* The Grand Manan Museum, The Provincial Archives of Nova Scotia, The Provincial Archives of New Brunswick, *The Canadian Encyclopedia,* Second Edition, Hurtig Publishers, Edmonton, 1988, (Atlantic Coast: *List of Lights, Buoys and Fog Signals,* Canadian Coast Guard, Aids and Waterways), *Saturday Evening Post, Journal of Education.*

East Ironbound Lighthouse, circa. 1920. *PANS N-7006.*

The Author

After graduating from High School, Chris Mills took a seamanship course at the Nova Scotia Nautical Institute and spent part of a summer as a trainee deckhand on an offshore supply ship. In 1988, he graduated from the University of King's College with a BA (Hons) in History.

The author has travelled in Great Britain, France, Germany, Greece, Italy, Switzerland and Norway. He has a strong interest in the sea, Maritime history, islands and coastal settlements. He has spent many summers on islands: Sable, Seal, Brier, and smaller islands along the shores of Nova Scotia, as well as islands abroad—the Outer Hebrides, Lindisfarne and Bass Rock.

At present he is considering a career in journalism, while working on a second book on the reminiscences of old lightkeepers. He divides his time between Ketch Harbour, N.S. and Gannet Rock, where he is an assistant keeper.